Robert Ellis

Asiatic Affinities of the old Italians

Robert Ellis

Asiatic Affinities of the old Italians

ISBN/EAN: 9783337385507

Printed in Europe, USA, Canada, Australia, Japan

Cover: Foto ©ninafisch / pixelio.de

More available books at **www.hansebooks.com**

THE
ASIATIC AFFINITIES

OF

THE OLD ITALIANS.

BY

ROBERT ELLIS, B.D.,

FELLOW OF ST. JOHN'S COLLEGE, CAMBRIDGE, AND AUTHOR OF "ANCIENT
ROUTES BETWEEN ITALY AND GAUL."

"Tuscos Asia sibi vindicat."

LONDON:
TRÜBNER AND Co., 60, PATERNOSTER ROW.
1870.

CONTENTS.

CHAPTER I.
PAGE

Migrations of the Aryans from their original home in Mount Imaus—Route of the Thracians into Europe—Western and Northern limits of the Thracian area in Europe—With what nations the Thracians came into collision—Primitive population of the South of Europe, and of Asia Minor and Armenia 1

CHAPTER II.
Etruscan sepulchral inscriptions 26

CHAPTER III.
Etruscan votive inscriptions 78

CHAPTER IV.
The Inscription of Cervetri 95

CHAPTER V.
Conjugations and Numerals 114

Index of Etruscan words, with their meaning 153

ERRATA.

In p. 15, l. 17; p. 16, l. 1; and p. 18, l. 24; for *Mœsia* read *Mœsia*.
In p. 94, l. 4; for *sulthn* read *salthn*.
In p. 102, l. 27; for *mataram* read *mataraṁ*.

PREFACE.

THE publication of the great work of Fabretti, the *Corpus Inscriptionum Italicarum*, has rendered available a rich store of materials for investigating the affinities of the ancient languages of Italy. The additional Etruscan epitaphs, in particular, are of the highest importance, and have induced me to return once more to the subject of the Etruscan language; for it does not appear, at least to my knowledge, that all the results to which the new inscriptions lead have hitherto been deduced from them. What the significance of those results is may be estimated from the facts, that we are now in possession of the written forms of several Etruscan numerals, that we are enabled to recognise the Etruscan equivalents for the Latin *-ginta* and *-genti*, and that, in addition to the previously known *ril*, "year," we may likewise elicit the Etruscan words for "month" and "day."

The objects which I have chiefly had in view in the following pages are: to demonstrate the Armenian character of the Etruscan language in as complete and brief a manner as possible, and to present such a vocabulary of Etruscan words as may be sufficient for the interpretation of the common forms of expression on the monuments of Etruria. It would increase the interest with which these relics of an ancient nation are regarded, if the meaning of the inscriptions which they bear could be understood, and we were thus qualified to know what the Etruscans engraved upon their offerings to the gods, and on the tombs of their dead. At the same time, these votive and sepulchral forms, when combined with the Inscription of Cervetri, and with such other points of evidence as may conveniently be introduced in connexion with these three bodies of proof, seem quite sufficient to disclose the nature of the language of the Etruscans, and thus to determine who that enigmatical people really were.

But the origin of the Etruscans is a question that does not stand alone, and that cannot be treated without touching on several others which relate to ancient and prehistoric times. To one of these in particular I have endeavoured to direct inquiry. As the Armenians, the last representatives of the old Thracian race at the present day, have been neglected or overlooked in all investigations relating to the affinities of the Etruscans; so too a similar extension, in remote ages, of the race of nations now confined to the Caucasian regions, is a probability that has not been sufficiently allowed for in constructing the population of Europe before the Aryans entered it. There seems, as far as I can judge, to be no necessity for inferring the extinction of either of the two ancient stocks mentioned eighteen years ago by Dr. Latham in the following passage, which sets forth very clearly and forcibly the two principal questions whose solution I have attempted :—

" The displacements effected by the different European populations, one with another, have been enormous. See how the Saxons overran England, the Romans Spain and Gaul. How do we know that some small stock was not annihilated here? History, it may be said, tells us the contrary. From history we learn that all the ancient Spaniards were allied to the ancestors of the Basques, all Gaul to those of the Bretons, all England to those of the Welsh. Granted. *But what does history tell us about Bavaria, Styria, the Valley of the Po, or ancient Thrace?* In all these parts the present population is known to be recent, and the older known next to not at all. The reconstruction of the original populations of such areas as these is one of the highest problems in ethnology. To what did they belong, *an existing stock more widely extended than now,* or a fresh stock altogether?"

"My own belief is, that the number of European stocks for which there is an amount of evidence sufficient to make their extinction a reasonable doctrine is two—two and no more; and even with these the doctrine of their extinction is only *reasonable.*"

"*a.* The old Etruscans are the first of these";

"*b.* The Pelasgi the second."

If the Etruscans were of the same race as the Armenians, and the Pelasgi of the same race as the Caucasians, both these stocks would still survive. The Caucasian tribes include the Georgians (with the Lazians and Mingrelians), who are connected through the Suanians with the Circassians and Abkhasians; the Ossetes, who are frequently supposed to be Aryans; the Kisti, who are connected through the Tuschi and

Pschawi with the Georgians; and the Lesgi in the ancient Albania. The languages of these tribes differ very considerably, but something common is found to run through them all.

The following equivalents will be employed for the Armenian alphabet; and the Greek letters which correspond to the Armenian in place, though not always in sound, are prefixed to them:—

a. a.
β. b.
γ. g.
δ. d.
ε. e (e or ye).
ζ. z (English z).
η. é.
ē (e mute).
θ. th (Hebrew tuth).
ž (French j).
ι. i.
l.
kh (guttural).
ẓ (ds).
κ. k.
h.
ṣ (ts).
λ. t (Welsh ll: Polish t).
ǧ (dž: English j).

μ. m.
y.
ν. n.
ξ. š (English sh).
ο. o.
č (tš: English ch).
π. p.
g̃ (dš: as sch in mensch).
ρ. ṛ (strong r).
σ. s.
w (strong v).
τ. t.
r.
ẓ̈ (tz: Hebrew tzaddi).
υ. v.
φ. ph (like p'h).
χ. ch (Hebrew koph).
ω. ó (broad o, or au).
f (used in foreign words).

ARMENIAN DIPHTHONGS.

av, the older form of ó.
ev, like English yew.
iv, vowel y, French u.

ov, vowel u, English oo.
ow, long o.
ea, like French è.

The Armenian alphabet was invented about 1500 years ago.

THE ASIATIC AFFINITIES OF THE OLD ITALIANS.

CHAPTER I.

Migrations of the Aryans from their original home in Mount Imaus.—Route of the Thracians into Europe.—Western and Northern limits of the Thracian area in Europe.—With what nations the Thracian race came into collision.—Primitive population of the South of Europe, and of Asia Minor and Armenia.

As the Asiatic element in Italy was mainly Etruscan, and the Aryan character of the Etruscan language will be apparent as soon as its examination is commenced, such an examination may be appropriately preceded by a sketch of the probable course of the Etruscans from the original home of the Aryan family of nations, and by an endeavour to determine what were the elements which composed the early population of the South of Europe.

A remarkable light has been thrown on the first movements of the Aryans by the researches of German scholars, the result of which is readily accessible in the third volume of Bunsen's *Egypt's Place in Universal History*. But the map which is there given as illustrating the "track of the Aryans from the Primeval Country to India," might perhaps receive with more justice the title of "a map to illustrate the tracks of the *Southern* Aryans from the Primeval Country to India and *Armenia.*" The "Primeval Country" was the mountainous region which contains the sources of the Oxus and the Jaxartes: and the map exhibits clearly how the Aryans, starting from this country, settled successively in Sogdiana, Margiana, Bactria, Parthia, Aria, and other tracts, until the list of the districts which they occupied in the earliest times concludes at last with these three countries:—

14. Varena, now *Ghilan*, S.W. of the Caspian.
15. Hapta-Hindu, now the *Punjab*.
16. "The sixteenth country has no specific name. Its inhabitants are the dwellers *near the sea-coast, who do not require any ramparts.* Their curses are *winter* and *earthquakes.* As the *Caspian* was the sea nearest to the Old Iranians, we must understand the shores of that sea."

It seems a highly probable inference that this last country was Armenia, which formerly touched *Ghilan* and the *Caspian Sea,** is protected by the natural *ramparts* of its mountains, has a long and severe *winter* on account of its elevated position, and is notoriously subject to *earthquakes.*† But, even with-

---

* See the map in Whiston's *Moses Choronensis.*

† "In the summer of 1840 Armenia was visited by a violent earthquake, which shook Ararat to its foundation. The immense quantities of loose stones, snow, ice, and mud, then precipitated from the great chasm, immediately overwhelmed and destroyed the monastery of St. James and the village of Arghuri, and spread destruction far and wide in the plain of the Araxes. Although

out this inference, the mention of Ghilan immediately before the Punjab, and the positions of the other thirteen regions previously named, would lead up to the following conclusion :—

The Southern Aryans, proceeding from the banks of the Oxus, and expanding as they advanced, reached Armenia on the west about the same time as they occupied the Punjab on the east, and before they entered Southern Media, Persia, Carmania, Gedrosia, and India beyond the Sutlej.

Whatever may be the historical value of these results thus deduced from the Vêndidâd, they fall in at any rate singularly well with the theory which I desire to support, and which may be stated in this manner:—

The Southern Aryans were ultimately divided into three principal stocks: the Thracian on the west, the Medo-Persian in the centre, and the Indian on the east. The Thracian race, as a distinct member of the South Aryan family, had its origin in Armenia, about the same time, and in the same manner, as the Indian race had its origin in the Punjab. Finally, while the Medo-Persians were gaining possession of the southern half of Iran, upon the Indian Ocean and the Persian

---

Ararat is formed of volcanic rocks, yet no allusion to its volcanic activity at any period, no mention of an eruption, is made by any of the native historians, who record, nevertheless, several earthquakes more or less calamitous." Appendix to Cooley's translation of Parrot's *Journey to Ararat*, p. 371. The earthquake of 1840 was felt as far as Tiflis, 150 miles N. of Ararat, and as Tauris or Tabreez, 150 miles S.E. of Ararat, near Ghilan.

Gulf, and while the Indians were carrying the Sanskrit language with them from the Indus to the Bay of Bengal, *the Thracians were extending themselves from the Caspian to the Alps and the Tyrrhenian Sea, and carrying an Armenian dialect into Etruria and Rhætia.*

That there were Thracians over all this extent of country is, however, not merely a probable or possible conjecture: it is a matter of ancient history, or at least of ancient tradition. What the earliest Zoroastrian record seems to exhibit in the germ, the authors of Greece and Rome present in its completion. Twenty-two such authors, as Mr. Donnis has noticed, derive the Etruscans from the Lydians; a presumption of affinity not to be hastily set aside, although the voyage of the Lydians to Etruria under the conduct of Tyrrhenus may be no more historical than the voyage of Æneas, and Tyrrhenus himself a personage like Hellen and Romulus, or Delphinus and Sabaudus, the sons of Allobrox. That some Alpine nations, and especially the Rhætians, were akin to the Etruscans, is a fact attested by Livy: and that the Lydians and Carians were allied in blood and language to the Mysians, who were a branch of the Thracian race, is affirmed by other writers. There were too, as we learn from Strabo, Thracians mixed with the Celtic inhabitants of Noricum and Pannonia, the countries which interveno between Rhætia and Dacia. The rest of the historical argument for the extension of the Thracians from Armenia to Italy may be summed up in the words of Dr. Latham, although he has rejected the result which

I not only accept, but extend to Etruria:* "The old Thracian affinities are difficult, but not beyond investigation. A series of statements on the part of good classical authors tell us, that the Daci were what the Getæ were, and the Thracians what the Getæ; also, that the Phrygians spoke the same language as the Thracians, and the Armenians as the Phrygians. If so, either the ancient language of Hungary must have been spoken as far as the Caspian, *or the ancient Armenian as far as the Theiss.*" Write here *the Alpine Rhine and the Tiber* for *the Theiss*, and I believe that no more than the truth would be said, and perhaps not quite as much as the whole truth. For I imagine that the Bebryces, whom several authors mention in the Eastern Pyrenees, were Thracian settlers who came thither by sea, probably from Italy, before the Carthaginians and Greeks formed settlements upon that line of coast. My reasons for this conjecture may be thus briefly expressed, as a part of the cumulative proof of the western extension of the Thracian race:—

Armenian... { *sarn,* "ice:" root *sar,* "freeze."
  patel, "to enclose" (th. *pat*).
  patovar, "wall, rampart."
Bithynia.......*Patavium,* a town of the Thracian Bebryces.
Pannonia......*Patavium,* a town, now *Pettau.*

---

* *Ethnology of Europe,* p. 229 (1852). Dr. Latham considers that two languages were spoken in Phrygia; one allied to that of the Armenians, and the other to that of the Thracians, whom he regards as Slavonic.

Venetia .... *Patavium,* the chief town, now *Padua.**
E. Pyrenees ... *Bebryces.*†
Pyrenees ...... *sern-eille,* "glacier." For the termination, compare *ab-eille, sor-ella,* and *or-illa.* The rest is Armenian. Observe, too, that *Iberians* bordered on these Bebryces, and on the Armenians.

Patavium, the chief town of Venetia, seems to have a Thracian and Armenian name. Of the Venetian language I know only one word, which is given by Pliny (*H. N.,* xxvi, 6): "*Halus* autem, quam Galli sic vocant, Veneti *cotonram.*" *Cotonea* "comfrey, σύμφυτον, *wallwurz,*" may be explained, like the Dacian κοτίατα, "ἄγρωστις, gramen," from the Armenian *khot,* "herb, forage," an Armenian word which nearly replaces the English *wort* and the German *wurz* in names of herbs. The Armenian *khotan,* "low, *humilis,*" shows a connexion in senso between *khot* and *humus.* Ptolemy mentions an Armenian town called Κόταινα. The *Cot-ensii* were a Dacian tribe.

The Bebryces in Roussillon, with the word *serneille,* "glacier," would mark the extreme western extension of the Thracians. On the north-west their limit would have been Rhætia, where their presence is indicated by several Rhæto-Romance words used in the Swiss Canton of the Grisons. The following group

---
* These three *Pataria*, and no others, are mentioned by Ptolemy.
† See Bouquet, *Historiens de la France,* vol. i, pp. 94, 114, 531, 677.

of five kindred terms may mark how the Southern Aryans once reached from the Ganges to the sources of the Rhine, while the existence in Lydian of the termination of the Armenian present participle, -*avt*, *ót*, or *ot*, is one sign that the Lydians had a more intimate degree of affinity with the Armenians than with the Indians. The Etruscan language, when we come to examine it, will exhibit exactly the same degrees of affinity to the Armenian and the Sanskrit that the ancient Lydian and Rhætian appear to have possessed. These are the five words:—

Sanskrit......... *kantha*, "the throat, the throttle."
Armenian........ *khetdavt*, "throttling, choking."
Lydian .... κανδαύλ-ης, "σκυλλοπνίκτης, the quinsy."*
Albanian........ *kyendis*, "I choke."†
Rhæto-Romance.. *candarials*, "a choking disease."‡

The following Rhæto-Romance names of animals exhibit also Armenian affinities:—

Guis, "marten." Armenian *kovz*, "pole-cat;" *kznachis*, "marten," = Polish and Bohemian *kuna*, Russian *kuniza*, Lithuanian *kiaune*.

Asöl, asoula, "kid." Armenian *ayz*, "goat" (= Sanskrit *ajá*, Greek αἴξ); *ovl*, "kid."

Turna, "moth." } Armenian *thithern*,
Fafarinna, "butterfly." } "butterfly."

---

* Bötticher's *Arica*, p. 44.   † Hahn's *Albanesische Studien*.
‡ "Eine Art Drüsenübel, das das Athmen sehr erschwert." Carisch's *Rhäto-Romanisches Wörterbuch*.

Salipp, "locust." Sanskrit *çalabha,* "locust:" root *çal,* "to run." Armenian *satap,* "quick, gliding."

There are thus signs of the Armenian language having once stretched as far as the Pyrenees and the Alps: and the same may be said of the Carpathians, for the relics of the Dacian language exhibit some striking instances of Armenian affinity. These relics consist of more than thirty names of plants used in medicine;* names that are very likely to contain the Dacian equivalents for the German *kraut* and *wurz,* and the English *grass, wort,* or *weed,* which are the terms that most commonly enter into the composition of German and English names of plants. The corresponding terms in Armenian are: *khot,* "herb, verdure, hay," and *det,* "herb, medicine, poison." Thus "tobacco" is *zkhakhot,* "smoke-herb," and "rhubarb" is *khasndet,* "flock-wort," in Armenian. Are there any indications of kindred words in Dacian?

Now ἄγρωστις, *gramen,* was called in Dacian κοτ-ίατα or κοτ-ήατα, in which we may fairly recognise the Armenian *khot,* "herb, hay;" while it is very probable that a word similar to the Armenian *det,* "herb, medicine, poison," existed in the Dacian διέλ-εια or διέλ-λεινα, "henbane;" τευ-διλά or τευ-δειλά, "calamint;" δουω-δηλά, "origan;" πρια-δῆλα or πρια-διλά, "black briony;" κοικο-διλά (or possibly κυκο-λίδα), "nightshade;" and perhaps προπε-δουλά or προπε-διλά "cinquefoil." In addition to *khot,* the Armenian has

---

* Grimm, *Geschichte der Deutschen Sprache,* cc. 9, 30.

another word for "grass," *séz*, apparently = Sanskrit *çáka*, "herba." This word, combined perhaps with the Armenian *anyağ*, "unlucky, detrimental," may be found in the Dacian ἀνιασσεξέ, "onobrychis:" Pliny (xxiv, 113) speaks of a plant called *impia herba*. There is too in Armenian the word *ost*, "ramus, germen, palmites, frondes" (cf. Basque *ost*, "leaf," and German *ast*), which, when combined with the Armenian *zow*, "θάλασσα," gives a good explanation of the Dacian ζουόστη, "artemisia," of which Dioscorides says that it grows for the most part ἐν παραθαλασσίοις τόποις. There is a fifth Armenian word of the same class as *khot, det, séz,* and *ost*, which are all apparently found in Dacian. This word is *phthith*, "the blowing of a flower," which gives the verb *phthēth-il*, "to blow, to bud, to sprout," with the present participle *phthēth-ot*, the preterite participle *phthēth-eal*, and the future participle *phthēth-eli*. We meet likewise with *phthith*, when combined with *zatik*, "flower," *mist*, "always," and *loys*, "light," in the following compounds:—

zatk-a-phthith, "flowering, blooming."
mēst-a-phthith, "ever-blooming."
lovs-a-phthith, "luminous, light-shedding."

To these add one of the previous Armenian *l* terminations, or such a one as in *ovś-et*, "sensible," from *ovś*, "sense," and then compare the Dacian—

φιθ-ο-φθεθελά, "ἀδίαντον, maidenhair."*

---

* Φιθ- is perhaps to be found in the Armenian *phet-ovr*, "feather."

It has been pointed out by Grimm that one Dacian word, κρουστάνη, "χελιδόνιον μέγα," is the Lithuanian kregždyne, and that another, δύν, "urtica, κνίδη," is the Welsh *dan-ad*. The existence of such words in Dacian may, however, be accounted for by contiguity of position; an expedient which cannot be admitted as an explanation of the Armenian affinities of the Dacian, which are, besides, more numerous and intimate than any other. There were Celts in Pannonia, and there may have been Lithuanians in Galicia; but Armenia is far away from Hungary and Wallachia.

Having now ascertained, by the combined aid of history and language, the probable limits of the Thracian area in Europe, we must proceed to consider another subject before entering upon the examination of the Etruscan language. What nations possessed the area in question when the Thracians first intruded upon it?

I spoke of Bunsen's map (*ante*, p. 2) as illustrating the tracks of the *Southern* Aryans to India and Armenia; for it is hardly probable that all the Aryans entered Europe through Armenia and Asia Minor. If the "Primeval Country" of the Aryans was the region where the Oxus and the Jaxartes have their sources, then another branch of that race, who may be called the Northern Aryans, would most likely take their way into the West along the north of the great barrier of sea and mountain, a thousand miles in

---

and *phet-tel*, "to pluck." Φιθοφθιθελλ would then be "feather-sprouting, plumy," just as the Armenian *lovsophthlilh* is "light-sprouting, luminous."

length, which is formed by the Caspian, the Caucasus, and the Euxine. The leaders of this division seem to have been the nations of the Classical stock, such as the Umbrians, the Oscans, and the Hellenes; which last I think, with Dr. Latham, to have been maritime settlers from Italy, as the Pelasgians and the Leleges may have come from Asia. I should find the explanation of *Pelasgi*, who are described as *veteres*, as αὐτόχθονες, as ἀρχαιότατοι, and as ἀρχαῖον τι φῦλον, in the Armenian words, *wat azg*, "ἀρχαῖον φῦλον;" where *azg* is "race, nation," and *wat* is "ancient, old," = Greek παλ-αιός, = Epirot πέλ-ιος. *Pelasgi* would be a Thracian term corresponding to the Greek *Autochthones* and the Latin *Aborigines*. Armenian words similar to *Pelasgus* in formation are: *lavazgi*, "noble," = *good-race*; *watazgi*, "plebeian," = *bad-race*; *azatazgi*, "citizen," = *free-race*; *aylazgi*, "foreigner," = *other-race*; and some more. *Leleges*, "again," is readily explained as "sailors," from the Armenian *let, lot, lovt*, "swim," *lotak* or *lovtak*, "swimmer;" *nava-lovtak*, "navigating."* The Classical nations would probably, as might be expected from the level nature

---

* "The *headlands* of Southern Greece, and some other parts of the *coast*, were occupied in the earliest times by the *Leleges* and other tribes, *which spread themselves from the opposite shores of Asia Minor over the islands of the Ægean Sea*. But, with these exceptions, the whole continent, from the borders of Thrace and Macedonia to the extreme point of Peloponnesus, was peopled by the great Pelasgian nation" (Malden). If the Leleges came by sea into Greece, and the Bebryces by sea into Roussillon, the Tyrrhenians *might* have come by sea into Etruria.

of their supposed route from the Oxus to the Danube, reach Italy before the Thracians, while the reverse may have been the case in Greece; and they would have been followed or accompanied into Europe by their kindred the Celts, till the Alps, or perhaps the Carpathians, severed the stream into a northern and a southern arm. The Celts, in their turn, would have been followed by the Germans, and the Germans finally by the Slavonians and Lithuanians; although it is possible that these two ramifications of the Sarmatian branch of the Aryan stock, whose languages have several Armenian affinities, may have preceded the Thracians through Asia Minor. I do not, however, think so myself. If the Thracians entered Europe from Asia Minor, and the Celts through the South of Russia, it might be anticipated that the two races would clash and mingle on the Lower Danube; and this would account, not only for what Celtic may appear in Dacian, but also for such Celtic words as the Etruscan has taken up.

But other tongues, besides the Celtic or any other Aryan language, may have affected the original Thracian as it was carried from Armenia to Etruria. Europe would have been peopled by some other nations before the Aryans entered it. Now, if we eliminate from Europe, together with that part of Asia which lies between the Caspian and Ægean Seas, all Aryan, Semitic, and Turkish inhabitants, we shall be left with only three races, or groups of nations: the Basques in the west, the Fins in the north, and the nations of the Caucasus in the east. The first approximation therefore that we should make towards reconstructing the primitive population of Europe (with Armenia and Asia Minor) would be, by extending the Basques, the Fins, and the Caucasians, till they met somewhere in the centre of Europe. I do not, however, find any linguistic signs of a Basque population there, though the Taurine *asia*, "rye," has been compared with the Basque *aciù*, "seed;" and the name of the Taurine *Iria*, now Voghera, is like the Basque *iria* or *uria*, "city." But I must notice three Alpine words which deserve attention as possible indications of an extension of Fins and Caucasians into those mountains. The Ossetes and Tuschi, it has been mentioned in the preface, are two Caucasian tribes; and the *Tuschi* would apparently be a remnant of those *Tusci* whom Ptolemy speaks of in Asiatic Sarmatia on the north slope of the Caucasus. It might be an extension of the same race that brought the *Tuscan* name into Europe, where we meet with it in Etruria. The three Alpine words are:—

1. *Küss, kees, käse*, "glacier" (Noric Alps).* Lapponic *kaisse*, "mons altior, plerumque nive tectus." Esthonian *kahho*, "frost; *kasse jää (jäa,* "ice"), "ice formed by frost upon snow." Georgian *qiswa*, "frost."†

2. *Laui, lauwi, lawine*, "avalanche."‡ Tuschi *law*, "snow" (Schiefner's *Thusch-Sprache*).

---

* The Noric Alps lie to the north of the great valley of the Drave, the Carnic Alps to the south.
† Compare the Peruvian *cassa*, "hail." Helps' *Life of Pizarro*.
‡ In Rhæto-Romance, *lavinna*.

3. *Tüssel*, "hoy, *knabo*" (Splügen district). Carian τουσσύλοι, "Πυγμαῖοι." Ossetic *tyūsül*, "little," = Armenian *doyzn*. Armenian *thzovk*, "a pygmy;" root *thiz*, "a span." Κάτ-τουζα, πόλις Θράκης, ἐν ᾗ κατῴκουν οἱ Πυγμαῖοι.*

The last of these three words may possibly be Aryan, and have been carried into Rhætia by the Thracians; but of the other two, one seems Caucasian, and the other both Finnish and Caucasian. There would be two explanations of the presence in the Alps of Turanian words for "ice" and "snow," if it may be allowable to apply the title "Turanian" to the Fins and Caucasians. Such words may have been taken up in Asia by the Thracians, and have been brought by them to Rhætia; or they may be due to an original Turanian population extending from the Ural or the Caucasus to the Alps. If we adopt, as I should be inclined to do, the second of these alternatives, we might be led to inquire if there were any European nations in historic times who belonged to this primitive Turanian population. That the Basques or Iberians formed a part of it is no improbable supposition; and I suspect that both they, and all the original inhabitants of the South of Europe, as well as of Asia Minor and Armenia, were allied in blood and language to the Caucasian nations, while the North of Europe, beyond the Alps and the Carpathians, would have been Finnish.† The identity of names is remarkable. Not

---

* Bötticher's *Arica*, p. 5.
† "The population of the first period," says Mr. Troyon, in his

merely were there *Iberians* and *Tuscans* in the Caucasus as well as in Spain and Italy; but the name of the nation which intervened in Europe between the Iberians and Tuscans, namely, the *Ligyes* or *Ligurians*, is found likewise in or near the Caucasus, as we know from Herodotus and Zonaras. There were, too, *Ligyrii* in Thrace, and the Taurisci of Noricum bore the additional name of *Ligyrisci*. The Ligurians of Italy were almost extirpated in their long war with the Romans (Niebuhr), and both in Italy and Gaul they would have been much Celticised, as we know that the Salyes were; while the Tuscans of Italy, if originally Caucasian, would have been conquered by the Thracian Rasenæ, and have lost their national existence, while they communicated, like the Britons, their name to their conquerors. The same lot probably befell the primitive population of Dacia and Mœsia; for, though the Dacian language was Thracian in the time of Dioscorides, as may be inferred from its Armenian affinities, and as Strabo had declared at a rather earlier period, yet the Dacian town-name *dava*, of which a few

---

work on the Swiss Lake-dwellers, "are a primitive people, perhaps belonging to a Finnish or Iberian race which came out of Asia several thousand (hundred) years before our era, and following the course of the Rhone or the Rhine wandered into the valleys of the Alps." Keller's *Lake Dwellings* (Eng. trans.), p. 395. I imagine that *law-ine* and *kees* are relics of the language of this Finnish or Iberian race, using *Iberian* in the double sense of Georgian (or Caucasian) and Basque; like as the ancient presence of the Thracian Bebryces in Roussillon would be indicated by the word *sern-eille*, "glacier," in the Pyrenees.

instances are found in Mæsia besides, with one in Dalmatia, and one in Dardania, seems best explained from the Georgian *daba*, "village, town," though probably allied at the same time to the Sanskrit *deça* and the Armenian *deh*, "pagus." A parallel might be made with Cornwall, where Celtic place-names exist among a people now speaking English. The *Daci* or *Davi* were probably "the villagers," as Gesenius has interpreted the name of the Caspian *Dahæ* or *Dai*.*

---

* The Georgian *daba* might also explain the name of the Galatian *Tavium*, and the last part of *Pa(t)-tavium* (ante, p. 5), while *Pat-* was referred to the Armenian *pat-el*, "to enclose." There was a Dacian town called *Patav-issa*. Two more Dacian towns were called *Acidava*, which bears a resemblance to *Acitavones*, the second name of the Centrones in Savoy. We know that there were the pile-towns of an early race on the Leman Lake—

"Quam vetus mos Græciæ
Vocitavit *Accion*." (AVIENUS)

Guadix in Andalusia was anciently called *Acci*. In Georgian, *vake* is "plain, fields," like the Spanish *vega*. In Lapponic, *wagge* is "valley;" "*imprimis vallis inter montes latior*," which would well describe the position of the Ligurian *Vagienni*. The Genoese *lalla*, "aunt," seems Finnish too, as *lel* is "uncle" in Esthonian. We find in Avienus the inhabitants of the Alpine valley of the Rhone called *Tylangii, Daliterni, Chabilci*, and *Temenici*, instead of *Viberi, Seduni, Veragri*, and *Nantuates*; just as the *Acitavones* were also *Centrones*, and as the *Medulli* were also *Garoceli*. Each one of the six tribes between the Furca and the Mont Cenis had two names, and so likewise had the *Lacus Lemanus*. The Alps were perhaps not much Celticised before the movement which brought the Gauls into Italy. The *Chabilci* seem to have left their name to *Chabls* and the *Chablais*, which once included the Lower Vallais. There was a town called *Chabala* in the Caucasian Albania. *Temnus* was a mountain in Mysia.

THE OLD ITALIANS. 17

A part of the *Albanians*, the probable representatives of the ancient Illyrians, are still called *Toscans*; and both are Caucasian names, though the Albanian language is Aryan, as Bopp has shewn in his essay on that subject. Among many remarkable Albanian words, two may be selected on account of their significance. One of them, *diel* or *dil*, "sun," resembles the Georgian *dili* or *dila*, "morning," but would also be allied in root to the Albanian *di(tē)*, "day," = Latin *dies*, = Sanskrit *di(na)*, = Welsh *dyw*, = Armenian *tiv*. The Armenian plural form, *tich*, "age," i. e. "days," would imply *ti* in the singular as another form of *tiv*. The Sanskrit *diva*, "heaven," is likewise a kindred term; and the root is the Sanskrit *div*, "to shine." By taking this root into the Armenian, dropping the *v* as in the Sanskrit *dina* = *divana*, and adding one of the Armenian *l* terminations (*ante*, p. 9), the Albanian *diel* or *dil*, "sun," comes to mean "shining, bright." Yet *l* terminations are as characteristic of Georgian as they are of Armenian and Etruscan; and *dili* or *dila*, "morning," is a true Georgian derivative from the root, *di(v)*, "to shine." In Tuschi, too, "God" is *Dal*, which might be deduced from a similar root.

For from the root *div* the Sanskrit derives also *deva*, "God," = Armenian *dev*, "demon;" which words, when combined with the Armenian *werin*, "high" (shortened into *wern* in *wern-akan*, "celestial"), lead us at once to the Albanian *perndi* or *perēndi*, "God." The root of *werin* is the Armenian *wer*, "on high" (= Sanskrit *para*, "altus"), which gives in the

c

comparative *weragoyn,* "superior," and enables us to explain the Phrygian βερεκύνδαι, "δαίμονες," i. e. "the supreme spirits;" or else as "the most high," if δ is not radical. *Berecynthus* was also a mountain.*

The Armenian for "God" is *astovaç,* = Zend *açīvat,* "existentia (*açīu*) præditus."†

The Etruscan words for "Deity" are Aryan, like the Armenian and Albanian. They are, according to Classic reporters, *æsar,* "deus," and *αἰσοί,* "θεοί." *Aes-* or *ais-* is the Old Norse *ās,* "deus," the Armenian *ays,* "spirit, demon," and probably also the Gaelic *aos,* "fire, the sun," from which by the addition of *fear,* "bonus, vir," = Sanskrit *vara,* Armenian *ayr,* are derived the Gaelic *Aosar,* and the Irish *Aosar, Aesar,* "God," which Bopp compares with the Sanskrit *içvara,* "dominus," and *iç,* "dominari." The connexion between "dominus" and "sol" is shown in the Sanskrit *ina,* "dominus," = Irish *ion,* "sol." Yet we should expect the Sanskrit *iç* to become *ic* (= *ik*) in Gaelic. The Etruscan for "heaven," *falandum,* would be allied to the Persian *buland,* "high, heaven," and the Sanskrit *oland,* "in altum tollere."

Whatever the population may have been originally in Illyria, Dacia, and Mæsia, yet it seems eventually to have been either Aryan or Aryanised, as it would certainly have been in Thrace and Greece: but among the mountains in the heart of the peninsula a remnant of the original Turanian inhabitants may have been

---

* Other languages present signs of affinity here. See Diefenbach, *Lex. Comp.* s. v. *fairguni,* "berg."

† Böttieher's *Arica,* p. 63.

left in the Pæonians, with the dwellers on piles whom Herodotus describes on Lake Prasias; the kindred, perhaps, of the Swiss lake-dwellers who have of late excited general interest, and whom "Realmah" has made so popularly known. The Pæonians represented themselves, according to Herodotus, as a colony of the Teucrians from Troy, and their remains were certainly called *Gergithes* (v. 22), and probably dwelt at *Gergis*, *Gergithium*, or *Gergithus*, in the territory of Lampsacus (Strabo, p. 589). *Gergeti* is an Ossetic town in the centre of the Caucasus. The pile-dwellers on Lake Prasias cut their timber in Mount *Orbelus*, and the *Orbelians* were a princely family in Georgia.*

If there were people of Caucasian origin in Europe, it is not likely that Asia Minor would be without them. The most eminent nation here that I should be inclined to consider as Turanian and Caucasian would be the Lycians, whose language, which is neither Aryan nor Semitic in character, appears to me to present signs of such an affinity. I have discussed the question at some length in my *Armenian Origin of the Etruscans*, and shall only select a very few points for notice here. The Lycian term for "wife," *lade*, deserves consideration in the first place, and may be thus derived from the Caucasian by the aid of the Circassian and Lesgi languages:—

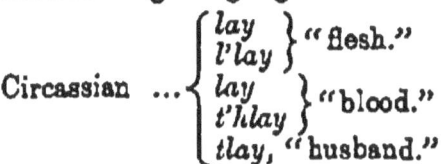

* St. Martin, *Mémoires sur l'Arménie*.

Lesgi ....*tly'adi* } "wife."
Lycian ....*lade*

Three other Lycian words are :—
tedé-eme, " son."
κάδρ-εμα, " σίτου φρυγμός."
ὖλ-αμος, " καρπός."

the last pair being two of the five Lycian words derived from Greek reporters. The terminations of these three words may be found in the termination of the Esthonian infinitive -*ma*, which resembles the Turkish infinitive terminations, -*mak*, -*mek*; or in the Tuschi noun-termination -*om*, which is, however, not common; or in the Lapponic noun-termination -*em*, which is exceedingly frequent: as, e. g.—*passat-et*, "lavare," *passat-em*, "lotio;"—*passot-et*, "colere," *passot-em*, "cultus;" *pass-et*, "assare," *pass-em*, "veru." But Aryan languages have similar terminations, as in ἄν-εμος.

For ὖλ-αμος we have—
Turkish *él-ma*   } "apple."
Hungarian *al-ma*

and for ὖλ- —
Esthonian *willi* } "fruit."
Tuschi *chil*

Georgian { *khili*, "apple."
{ *th-khili*, "nut."

for κάδρ- —
Tuschi *kotor*, "cake, bread."

and for *tedé*- —
Esthonian *toid-*   } "nourish."
Armenian *taz-*

Greek τήθη, "nurse."

I subjoin one Lycian epitaph to show the language, and because it will enable me to explain a word better than I did on a former occasion:—

ẽwuinu	gorũ	mute	prinafatũ	ẽsêdéplume	urppe
this	tomb	here	made	Esedeplume	for
lade	ẽuwe	sẽ	tedésaeme	ẽuweyẽ	womóleyẽ.
wife	his	and	children	his	all.

For the last word compare:—

Tuschi
{ wune.........." some, *was, welches.*"
wun—ele ..." every, *jedes.*"
wum........." something, *etwas.*"
wuma ......" all, *alles, alle.*"

Lycian ...*wom—ele—yẽ*, " all."

On a gold collar about six inches in diameter, which is now in the Museum of Vienna, and was found in Wallachia, a part of ancient Dacia, in the year 1838 (Micali, *Mon. Ined.*, tav. LIII), there is an inscription written from left to right, which may be read by the aid of the Lycian characters, *alufiithdi iifipfa*, "the *iifipfa* of Alufiithûs," a name partially like *Alyattes.** Here the short *a* is X, which is Lycian; and the *u*, I surmounted by X, which is also Lycian. If the X be made a χ or *ch* instead of a short *a*, the inscription would become *chlufiithdi iifipfch*, which seems a less likely reading. The remaining letters in the inscription have nothing particularly distinctive about them. If the collar were a votive offering, or even a gift to an individual, *iifipfa* might

---

* Pausanias (x, 16) says, that of all the offerings of the Lydian kings nothing remained at Delphi but the iron pedestal or base of the bowl of Alyattes.

be explained from the Tuschi *iphob* = Georgian *isphoba*, "generosity, munificence, *freigebigkeit*;" which consists of the Tuschi *iaph*, = Georgian *isphi*, "munificent," combined with the Tuschi termination *-ob* = Georgian *-oba*. Votive offerings are said to be given *libenter* and *libera munere*. Such a Georgian form as *saso-eba*, "hope," comes still nearer to *tif-ipfa*, though *-ipfa* should likewise be compared with the Sanskrit *çal-abha*, = Armenian *sat-ap*, = Rhæto-Romance *sal-ipy* (*ante*, p. 8).* We have seen from the Dacian *-dava*, = Georgian *daba*, "village, town," that the language of Dacia was probably at first Caucasian, and from the Dacian names of plants that it became afterwards Thracian; as the language of Gaul became Latin while the Celtic town-names were retained in the country. Yet it does not follow, because the gold collar was found in Dacia, either that its original destination was Dacia, or that the inscription on it is Dacian. It might have been carried off, and brought to Dacia. For the declension of *Alufiithai*, compare the Tuschi *Markai*, the genitive of *Mark*, "Marcus;" and *maśai*, the genitive of *maśa*, "lux," = Sanskrit *mâs*, "luna," = Georgian *mse*, "sol."

Micali thinks the characters on the Wallachian collar to be like the Euganean letters. The Euganeans may very well have been a remnant of the early Turanians of Italy. They were neither Gauls nor Venetians.

---

* Compare *apfel, hüpfen, kopf*, and *apple, hop, cop.*

Malden writes, in his unfinished, and hardly commenced, *History of Rome*: "The mountainous country northward from the lake (of Garda) remained in possession of the Euganei. Of this ancient and once powerful people Cato was still able to enumerate thirty-four towns (Plin. *H. N.* iii, 24); and they were reported by tradition to have inhabited all the country between the Alps and the Adriatic Sea, till they were driven into the mountains by the Veneti (Liv. i, 1). Their chief tribe was the Stoni or Stœni (Plin. *H. N.* iii, 24), and the Stœni are expressly named Ligurians in a fragment of the Triumphal Fasti, and by the geographer Stephanus." I think it probable that the Euganeans are rightly connected with the Ligurians, as well as the Orobii, whose origin Cato could not ascertain (Plin. *H. N.* iii, 23). The same mystery hangs over the origin of the Euganeans. Micali says (vol. ii, p. 25): "Vanamente però vorremmo rintracciare l'origine degli Euganei." No doubt it is difficult to do so. Indeed, until Caucasians or Fins be brought in, there is always one race at least, in Italy, in the Turkish peninsula, and in Asia Minor, which cannot be accounted for. The name of the *Orobii*, who occupied the mountains of Como, and possessed *Berg-omum* (which is like *Perg-amus*, and may contain a termination like the Tuschi -*om* and that of the Lycian ὑλ-αμος); of the river *Orobis*, now the *Orb* in Languedoc; of the river *Orba* in the Ligurian Apennines; of the Pæonian Mount *Orbelus*; and of the Georgian *Orbelian* family; —all these names may be compared with three given by Ptolemy: *Orbanassa* in Pisidia, and *Orbisene* and *Orbalissene* in Armenia Minor, where *-sene* would be the Armenian termination *sén*, found in *mezasén*, "great," and *sikasén*, "red." Cf. Tyr-*senus* and Por-*sena*. It signifies also "town," and is Georgian as well as Armenian. *Orbi* means "eagle" in Georgian, and *-ali* and *-eli*, which may appear in Orb-*elus* and Orb-*alissene*, are common Georgian terminations: e. g. dab-*ali*, "humilis," from *dab*-a, "pagus;" Guri-*eli*, "belonging to the country of Guria." *Mount Orbelus* would probably = *Adlersberg*, but the rivers *Orba* and *Orobis* would rather mean "swift," like as the Etruscan *aracus*, "hawk,". is the Armenian *arag*, "swift." Cf. *Araxes*. There is an *Arbel-horn* in the Berneso Alps.

The Tuschi call their own country *Baża* (Schiefner, s. v.); a name resembling the Hispanian *Basti*, now *Baza*, which Humboldt compares with the Basque *baso(a)*, "forest." The *Bessi* were a Thracian tribe.

There was an ancient people in Paphlagonia or Bithynia called *Caucones*, who were extinct in Strabo's time. Some thought them to be Scythians, others Macedonians, and others Pelasgians. A people of the same name were once found in Messenia and Elis. The *Cauco-ensii* were a Dacian tribe. Cf. *Caucasus*.

In addition to the Lycians, I should be inclined to consider as Caucasian the Pisidians and Lycaonians, neither of whom are mentioned as Thracians, though the Phrygians and Milyans, who bordered on them, are expressly said to be so. *Lycaon* was a son of *Pelasgus*. When the Thracians advanced from the

Caspian into Armenia and Asia Minor, I think that they left the relics of the primitive Caucasian population, on their right in Armenia, and on their left in Asia Minor. Upon the whole, I may define the position which I imagine the Caucasians held with respect to the Thracians, both in Asia and Europe, by comparing it to that which the Dravidas now hold with respect to the Sanskrit nations in India. The Cappadocians or White Syrians, who divided the Armenians from their kindred, the Phrygians, would have been Semitic invaders from the south at a later period, whom an infusion of Thracian and Caucasian blood may have rendered fairer in complexion than the rest of the Aramæans. As the Thracians proceeded from Asia towards the west, their language, previously liable to be affected with Caucasian and Semitic elements, would probably have taken up some Celtic, and perhaps some Finnish words, especially in Italy and the Eastern Alps. But its substance and its structure would remain Armonian; and such, I believe, the Etruscan language will prove on examination.

CHAPTER II.

ETRUSCAN SEPULCHRAL INSCRIPTIONS.

It has been shewn in the preceding chapter, from the accounts of the ancients, how they made a series of Thracian nations to extend from the Caspian Sea as far as the Carpathians and the sources of the Rhine; and several linguistic coincidences have been brought forward in confirmation of the truth of these accounts, which there does not seem to be any reason for impugning. There is then, as Etruria is included in the Thracian area, a certain antecedent probability that the Etruscan language would be found to belong to the same Aryan family as the Armenian: and we have, besides this, the evidence of Livy, a native of Padua, that the Rhætian language, which appears from its relics to have been like the Armonian, was Etruscan with a corrupt pronunciation. It will accordingly be the object of this and the two following chapters to show that the Etruscan language was Aryan of the Armenian type; and the argument will be opened by an examination of the Etruscan epitaphs that contain the often cited *avil* and *ril*, words both characterised by one of those *l* terminations to which I have already called attention.

There are three words, *ætas*, *annus*, and *vixit*, which continually occur in Latin epitaphs, accompanied by the name and age of the deceased. The case is the same in Etruscan, where the corresponding words are *avil*, *ril*, and *leine*, with *line* elsewhere. To illustrate the use of these Etruscan words, it will be sufficient to select the following seven of Lanzi's epitaphs, in each of which the proper name is omitted, and its place supplied, for convenience of reference, by the number of the epitaph:—

453. *avil* XXXIII.   454. *avil ril* LXV.
32. *avils* XXIX.   455. *ril* LIII *leine*.
10. *ril* XXI.   456. *ril leine* LV.
87. *line*.

There are almost enough materials here to determine the family of languages to which the Etruscan belonged, for the respective meanings of *avil*, *ril*, and *leine*, are scarcely to be mistaken. I will, however, as so much is to be learned from these three words alone, proceed to prove what a careful observer might very likely perceive on inspection: and this demonstration seems to be the more requisite, as it was said long ago, and has not yet entirely ceased to be repeated, that all we know of the Etruscan language is, that *avil ril* means "vixit annos," though it cannot be said which is the noun, and which the verb.* Even

---

* "Of their language, chiefly preserved to us in their sepulchral inscriptions, we know absolutely nothing. The only expression that has been satisfactorily made out is the very common one of RIL AVIL, 'vixit annos.'" Murray's *Central Italy*, p. 256 (ed. 1857).

Niebuhr was at fault here. "Al dire di lui," writes Micali, in his *Antichi Popoli Italiani* (vol. ii, p. 351), "la scienza dell' Etrusco sarebbe ristretta all' interpetrazione *certa* di due sole parole: AVIL RIL, *vixit annos*."

Yet all that can be pronounced certain, or almost certain, is, not that *avil ril* means "vixit annos," but that of the two expressions, *avil ril* and *ril leine*, one signifies "vixit annos," and the other "anno ætatis." *Ril* therefore, which occurs in both expressions, stands for both *anno* and *annos*, and would consequently be the Etruscan word for "year" used without declension, or else contracted to its crude form like *ann.* and *ætat.* in Latin. Again, as *avil* and *avils* cannot both be rendered "vixit," to say nothing of other obvious reasons, it is plain that *avil* is *ætas* or *ætat.*, and that *avils* is *ætatis;* so that *avil* would be declined like an Aryan noun. So far then from its being certain that *avil ril* means "vixit annos," it is easy to see that *avil ril* cannot mean "vixit annos." Finally, as *ril* is "year," and *avil* is "ago," no sense but "lived" is left for the remaining word *leine*, which, when accompanied by the number of years of life, is always joined with *ril*, "years," as *vixit* is with *annos.** When it stands alone, as *line*

---

* "Occurrit (*leine*) in titulis sepulcralibus (ex Volaterris), conjunctum cum voce *ril*, quod exponitur *annos* vel *annorum.*" Fabretti, p. 1042. Should it not therefore have been inferred that *leine* corresponded to "vixit," especially when *avils*, "ætatis," had been rightly interpreted, as it has for some time been in Italy? Of the explanations that have been given for *leine*, the Latin *lene*, i. e. *leniter*, and the Greek λεῖνος, are selected as the most probable in Fabretti's vocabulary. But even if *lene* be taken

does twice in Lanzi, the Roman euphemism, "she lived," would be employed for "she is dead."

The Etruscan words, *leine* or *line*, "he lived," *ril*, "year," and *avil*, "age," may be thus explained:—

SANSKRIT.

Root *li*, "adhere, dwell, *live*."
laya, "house, dwelling."*
lindti, "he dwells."
alindt, "he was dwelling."

ARMENIAN.

Root *li*, "become, be, live" (implied in *li-eal*, "been").
lavray or *lóray*, "dwelling, home."
Lórê or *Lori*, name of two towns, "*Ham*."
lini, "he is."
linér, "he was" (imperfect: there is no aorist).

ETRUSCAN.

Lori-um, name of a town.†
leine or *line*, "he lived."

---

as a valediction equivalent to "sit tibi terra levis," and Αδιτος as meaning "tumulus," how can the resulting explanations of *ril leine* LV or *ril* LIII *leine* be more probable than "annos vixit.."? There is no reason to infer at starting that the Etruscan, Greek, and Latin languages belonged to one family, but rather, as Niebuhr and Micali affirmed, strong grounds for separating the Etruscan from the other two: for the Greek and Latin, after being put to the torture for a century, have given no explanation of the commonest Etruscan forms. Proximity need not imply affinity; and the languages of Etruria and Latium may have been no more nearly allied than are those of England and Wales.

* Cf. Thracian λίβα, "πόλις." Bötticher's *Arica*, p. 51.
† *Loro* and *Lari* are two modern towns in Tuscany.

GAELIC.

Root rà, "go."
   rà-idh, "a quarter of a year."

SANSKRIT.

Root ri, "go."
   ri-tu, "a season (of two months)."

ARMENIAN.

Root ṛah, "go" (implied in ṛah-el, "to go").
   kath-il, "to drop, a drop" (root kath).

ETRUSCAN.

r-il, "a year." Compare n-il = nih-il.

SANSKRIT.

Root av, "grow, move."

ARMENIAN.

lin-il or lin-el, "to be" (root li, base lin).
lin-eli, "that is to be" (future participle).
av-eli, "exceeding, redundant, more."
yav-êt, "more, rather."
yav-itean, "an age."
av-ag, "more aged, elder."
tes-il, "aspect" (root tes).

ETRUSCAN.

av-il, "age."

The Armenian av-r, "day, time, age," and av-î, "ring," i. e. "circle, circuit, orbit," might also be akin to avil and the Sanskrit av: and the following words may be cited to illustrate the connexion between "going" and "year," and "season" and "year;" as well as to exhibit still further the relationship of the

Indians to the Armenians, and of both, in their proper degree, to the reputed ancestors of the Etruscans:—

SANSKRIT.

Root *hi*, " go, increase, amplify."
hayana, "year."

nava, "new."
çarad, " autumn, year;" whence *çârada*, "new."

ARMENIAN.

Nava-sard, "ancient name of first month:"
zardi, "new."

LYDIAN.

Νέος σάρδις, " New-year."*

OSSETIC.

särd, " summer."

Something may likewise be said about the forms of the Armenian words adduced to explain *leine, avil*, and *ril*. The Armenian imperfect is formed like the imperfect of the Latin *possum*, so that *lin-èr*, "he was living," corresponds to *pot-erat:* for the Sanskrit *âsît*, "he was," = Zend *âs*, = Armenian *èr*, = Latin *erat*.† But, in the imperfect, it is only in the third person singular, and there, it may be, in order to distinguish *èr*, "he was," from *é*, "he is," that the Armenian retains the *s* of the Sanskrit root, converted into *r* as in Latin. In the Armenian *èi*, "I was," = Sanskrit *âsam*, and *èir*, " thou wast," = Sanskrit

---

* Bötticher's *Arica*, p. 49. The city *Sardis* might derive its name from the Armenian *zardi*, "new." Cf. Ebrard on Rev. iii, 1.
† The augment is, however, wanting in *erat*.

ásis, that letter is omitted; so that we should rather expect in the third person, instead of *linér*, a form like the Etruscan *leine* or *line*, "he lived," which may, too, be the Sanskrit (*a*)*lin* (*t*), "he was living," when the augment is dropped, as in Latin, Zend, and Armenian, and the final *t*, as in Armenian, Greek, and Italian. But perhaps, as we shall see eventually, *leine* is an historic present, = Armenian *lini*, while *line* is the imperfect. With respect to *av-il* and *r-il*, it should be noticed, that -*il* is the usual termination of the passive or neuter infinitive in Armenian, as in *lin-il* (or *lin-el*), "to be." The Etruscan *ril*, "year," i. e. "course (of the sun)," would thus signify originally "das Gehen," = Armenian *ṛahel*, just as the Armenian *kathil* signifies "a drop," as well as "to drop:" and *avil*, "age," would in like manner signify "das Wachsen." The German *leben* is another example of an infinitive that is also a noun: and it is remarkable that a single Armenian word *lin-il*, "leben," should contain the meaning of *leine* or *line*, and the form of *av-il* and *r-il*. In the Etruscan *lein-*, too, there is a double affinity to the Sanskrit and Armenian; for the conjugational *n* is there, as well as the root *li* or *li*.

In the Armenian *lavray* or *lóray*, "a home," which explains the signification of the Armenian *Lori* and the Etruscan *Lori*-um (*ante*, p. 29), the root of dwelling, *li* or *li*, seems combined with the Sanskrit *vṛi*, "tegere," which occurs, with the termination -*an* added, in the Armenian *wran*, "tent, booth." Compare *Verona*, the Noric *Virunum*, and the village *Vrin* in the Grisons.

Avil or *avils*, "ætatis," accompanied by the number of years of life, is found in conjunction with two other words besides *ril*. One of these words appears in two forms, *lupu* and *lupuke*, the last being one of those *-ke* forms which are so common in Etruscan, as in *tur-ke* or *turu-ke*, "be gives." In Lanzi we find :—

465. *lupu*.
463. *lupu avil* XXIII.
464. *lupu avils* XVII.

and in Fabretti :—

2100. *avils* XXXVI *lupu*.
2058. *avils* LX *lupuke*.

If *avil ril* corresponds to *anno ætatis*, and *ril leine* to *vixit onnos*, the Latin form to which *lupu avils* corresponds would most likely be *obiit ætatis*. *Lupu* would then mean "he dies," and be a verb belonging to a *u* conjugation, like the Armenian *lizov*, "he licks." The root of *lup-u* is supplied by the Sanskrit *lup*, "destroy;" *lúp*, "kill, rob;" or by the Polish *tup*, "booty;" *tup-ić*, "to plunder;" *tup-ać*, "to split;" or by the Gaelic *lobh*, "putrefy," and the Irish *lubha*, "corpse." All these words are allied to the Sanskrit *lu*, = Greek λύ-ω, and to the Armenian *lovz-el*, "to loose." We shall meet in another epitaph with *lupum*, which means "corpse" in the accusative.*

I said it was only *almost* certain that *avil ril* and *ril leine* meant "anno ætatis" and "vixit annos," because it would be possible *a priori* that *lupu avils* meant

---

* The Greek and Latin explanations of *lupu* are λοῦδι and *locus*.

"vixit annos," and *ril leine*, "ætatis obiit." The forms might be sufficient to assure us that, in these four words, *ril* and *avil* are the two nouns, and *lupu* and *leine* the two verbs. If, therefore, we can deduce, from the Armenian and Sanskrit, *avil*, " age," *ril*, " year," *leine*, " ho lives," and *lupu*, " he dies," we should have the right meanings for the four words collectively, and might fairly conclude that each one of them was correctly interpreted. Nor would this conclusion be much, if at all, shaken, because *avil* with a number is found connected with one more word, as in the following epitaph, where the proper name is omitted as before (*Giorn. Arcad.*, vol. cxix, p. 325):—

zilachnke avil S.I. (qu. *avils* . .)

Orioli renders these words conjecturally, "obiit, depositus est, sepultus est ('o simile') ætatis —— ;" and it is not easy to see how a different meaning can be given to them. As, therefore, the sense "obit" (= "obiit") is in all probability anticipated by *lupu*, *zilachnke* ought apparently to mean " sepelitur, infoditur": and, as the Aryan character of the Etruscan is sufficiently apparent in the forms already interpreted, a root found in many Aryan languages would be an appropriate root for *zilachnke*. Such a root appears in the Greek λάκος, in the Gaelic *lag*, " cavum, specus," in the Italian *lacca*, "fossa, caverna," in the Armenian *ałag*, " fossa," and in the Phrygian *lachit*, which probably means "fodit." Assuming, then, *lach* as the Etruscan for "grave," and "is buried" as the meaning of *zilachnke*, we might make the following comparisons between Etruscan and Armenian forms:—

ETRUSCAN.

lach,............... " a grave."
zi—lach —nk— e, " he is buried."

ARMENIAN.

akn,............... " an eye."
z—akan————ê, " he eyes."
ett, ... " a place."
z—etet ———— ê, " he places."
getin, ... " ground, *terre*."
z—getn ———— ê, " *il terrasse*."
pholth,............ " a response."
phokh ———— ê, " he exchanges."
phokh—anak,... " change, lieutenant, vicar."
phokh—anak-ê, " he exchanges, he succeeds."
yatth, ... " great."
yatth ———— ê, " he conquers."
yatth—anak, ... " victory."
yatth—anak—ê, " he triumphs."

The only discrepancy here is, that the Etruscan *zilachnke* is passive, while the Armenian verbs cited are active; though *yatthanaké*, " he triumphs," and *phokhanaké*, " he succeeds," i.e. " he puts himself in the place of another," may be considered as reflective. In Armenian, *n* implies " self," and *k* is causative.

Z is prefixed to nouns and pronouns, as well as to verbs, in Armenian. It distinguishes the objective from the nominative: e.g. *sirel zAstovaz*, " to love God, *amar á Dios*." It also marks other cases: as— *erthal zoskvoy*, " to go *for* gold" (*oski*) ;—*arkanel znowav*, " to put *upon* him." On the whole, whether prefixed to verbs, where it is augmentative or determinative, or to pronouns and nouns, where it is the latter, its force seems nearly the same as that of ἐπί.*

In addition to *zilachnke avil..*, *lupu avils* XVII, and *avils* LX *lupuke*, we find in Fabretti (2059), *zilachnuke lupuke*, "infoditur, moritur,"—"he is dead and buried." This shews that *zilachnke* is not synonymous with *lupu* and *lupuke*, and can, therefore, hardly mean anything else than " he is buried" or " interred." If so, and tho root be *lach*, = Armenian *etag*, "fossa," the manner in which the Armenian enables us to build up *zilachnke* is very remarkable. As the Armenian *phokh* gives *phokhé* and *phokhanaké*, "he exchanges," we should first get *etaganaké*, " fodit(ur);" and, as *ett* gives *zetelé*, " he places," we should next get *zetaganaké*, "infodit(ur),"= *zilachnke* or *zilachnuke*.

I now come to nine epitaphs of the greatest value, as they contain Etruscan numerals, not in *figures*, but in *words*. I shall, therefore, give them at length, with their numbers in Fabretti :—

2104. Larthi Keisi Keises Velns Velisnas Ravnthus sech
avils sas Amke Uples.†

---

* The Armenian word *si*, = Zend *si*, = Sanskrit *hi*, signifies "for, *nam, denn*, γάρ."

† *Amke Uples* was probably the person who provided the tomb, or undertook the burial. See 2070 and 2340, where *Amke* seems the nominative to *kepen tenu* and *kisum tame*…, "offers the grave," and "buries the corpse." *Kepen* may be the accusative of a noun corresponding to the Armenian *gorb*, gen. *gěb-oy*, "a ditch, a cistern;" and *tenu* would be equivalent to the Armenian *tani*, "*tenet, tendit*." *Kisum*, as will be shown subsequently, may be the accusative of *kis-*, "a corpse," and *tame*...... "buries," appears

2119. Vipinanas Vel Kla
   ate Ultnas La(r)thal klan
   avils tivrs sas
2033 *bis*. Vel Leinies Larthial Ruka Arnthialum
   klan Vclasam prumaths *avils scsphs
   lupuke*
2071. Larth Churchles Arnthal Churchles Thanch-
   vilus(k) Krakial
   klan a*vils kiemzathrms lupu*
2070. Arnth Churkles Larthal klan Ramthas Pevtnial
   vilk Parchis Amke
   Maranach Sparana kepeu tenu *avils machs
   semphalchls lupu*
2340. Ramthn Matulnci sech Markvs Matulm ...
   puiam Amke Sethres Keis(in)ics kisam tame ... u
   Laf.nask Matulnask klalum*ke.s kiklena R.m.
   a .. *avenke lupum avils (m)achs mealchlsk*
   Eitvapia me...
2335a. Larth Arnthal Precas klan
   Ramth(a)s Apatrual eslz
   zilachnthas† *avils thunesi muvalchls lupu*
2335d. A..ikne ..eltna........turefnesithvas
   a *vils kis muvalchl*.......
2108. Vipinans Sethre Velthur .. Meklasial Thanchvilu
   a*vils kis kealch(l)s*

---

akin to the Armenian *damban*, "a sepulchre." *Ravnthus* (2104)
should probably be *Ramthas*, as 2070 and 2340 seem to shew: but
I shall not correct the proper names.

* *Klalum*, "mœrorem, funera." Greek κλαίω. Armenian *lal*,
"mourning, lamentation."

† Qu. *illachnuks*, "sepelitur."

In 2340, we meet with .. *avenks lupum* instead of *lupu*. This form must be explained before proceeding to analyse the numerals. The root of .. *avenke*, one of the Etruscan *-ke* forms, like *lupuke, turuke, turke*, and *erske*, would probably be the Sanskrit *av*, "servare," which is found in the Armenian *ap-avén*, "refuge ;" *ap-* being equivalent to the Sanskrit *apa, ap-*, and the Greek ἀπό, ἀπ-. *Apavini* means in Armenian, "he takes refuge, he consigns himself;" so that the active *apaviné* would mean "he consigns," and the Etruscan .. *avenke lupum* would be rendered "deponit corpus."

But .. *avenke* might, perhaps, be better explained, still keeping to the same root *av*, "servare," from the Armenian :—

avan(d),* "deposit, consignment."

avand-el, "to deposit, to give up.".

avandé zhogin, "he gives up the *ghost (hogi)*, he dies;" a singular parallel to the Etruscan .. *avenke lupum*, "he gives up the *body*, he dies."

I will notice at a later period the terms of parentage or descent in these epitaphs, *klan, sech*, and *puiam*, the accusative of *puia*, "filia." Their explanation is not necessary, as that of .. *avenke lupum* was, to prepare the way for the consideration of the numerals, to which we will now proceed. From the first three of the epitaphs we get :—

avils *sas*

avils *tivrs sas*

---

* Compare τέλος and tendo; also Armenian spand, "slaughter," from span, "kill;" and avan, "village" (= Sanskrit avani, "terra"), and sar-avand, "headland" (sar, "head").

avils *sesphs* lupuke
"ætatis ...... obit."

I need scarcely cite such forms as *avils* xxxvi *lupu* and *avils* lx *lupuke*, to prove that *sesphs*, in *avils sesphs lupuke*, is a numeral: but I must defer its consideration for the present, as Fabretti gives the reading as *sesphs* in the inscriptions, but as *semphs* in the vocabulary; and *semph*, as will be seen later, appears to be the Etruscan for "seven." In *avils sas*, and *avils tivrs sas*, *sas* would be "six," = Sanskrit *śaś*, = Persian *śaś*, = Lithuanian *szeszi*, = Latin *sex*, = Greek ἕξ, = Armenian *weṣ*, = Afghan *śbaź*, = Zend *khsvas*, = Ossetic *achsāz:* and *tivr-s* would be "thirty," = Welsh *tri-deg*, = Latin *tri-ginta*, = Lithuanian *trys-deszimtis*, = Sanskrit *trim-çat*, = Zend *thri-çata*, = Armenian *eresovn*, = Afghan *dér-ś*. This last form is very like the Etruscan, which should, perhaps, be *tior-s*, as *E* and *V (F)* are easily confounded.

We now pass to the fourth epitaph, which gives:—
avils *kiemzathrms* lupu
"ætatis .... obit."

This epitaph belongs, as is seen from the effigy, to an old man *(uomo vecchio)*, and would, therefore, involve "fifty," "sixty," "seventy," or even "eighty." If *kiemz-* be put by the side of *tivrs* or *tiors*, "thirty," it will be apparent that *kiem* may mean "five," and the following table will show how it ranges with other Aryan forms for that numeral:—

Sanskrit...*pañćan*
Persian...*pang*
Lithuanian...*penki*

Armenian { *hing*
{ *yi-*

Latin { *quinque*
{ *quin-*

Gaelic... *cuig*

Etruscan... *kiem*

Swedish... *fem*

Gothic... *fimf*

Welsh... *pump*

Greek { πέμπε
{ πέντε

Afghan... *pinza*

Kiemz- thus means "fifty," = Sanskrit *pañćúçat*, = Persian *pangáh*, = Afghan *panźús*, = Armenian *yisovn*, = Swedish *femtio*, = Gaelic *caogad*, = Latin *quinquaginta*, = Bohemian *padesat*. The termination of *kiemzathrms* would seemingly involve *thr-*, "three," = Sanskrit *tri*, = Zend *thri*, = Armenian *er* and *ere(ch)*, = Afghan *diré*: and *-m-* in *-thrms* might be the sign of the ordinal, as in the Latin pri-*mus* and the Lithuanian pir-*mas*, "fir-st," which Bopp compares with the Sanskrit para-*ma*, "eximius, summus." The final *s* in *kiemzathrms* would then mark the genitive, and the whole word would signify "(anni) quinquagesimi tertii." If so, there are five Aryan characteristics in *kiem-za-thr-m-s*.

The sihilants in *-s* and *-z*, "-ginta, -κοντα," would indicate that the Etruscan language did not belong to the same Aryan family as the Greek and Latin, and that it was not Coltic or Teutonic. In the Etruscan

-s or -z, tho n of tho Armenian -sown or -san, " -ginta," is dropped, as it is in the Afghan -ś or -s. There is the same omission in tho Ossetic düs, tho Hindustani des, tho Persian dah, and tho Welsh deg, "ten," which are all = Sanskrit daçan, Armenian tasn or tasan, Latin decem, Gothic taihun. This n is wanting also in the Sanskrit -çat and the Zend -çata, " -ginta;" hut an additional t suffix is introduced, as in Latin and Greek, of which the Etruscan and Armenian know nothing. The Old Slavonic has not only this t, hut retains besides, like the Teutonic languages, tho da of daça(n) in the Sanskrit -(da)çat, " -ginta." Thus tho Slavonic for "thirty" and "fifty" are tri-desjatj and pjatj-desjatj, which are very unliko tho Etruscan tier-s and kiem-z. The Lithuanian has trys-deszimtis and penkios-deszimtis for "thirty" and "fifty." The Etruscan problem seems thus nearly reduced to a choice between the Sanskrit and the Armenian; and if tho Sanskrit could he got rid of, the Armenian would then ho left alone. Another letter-change, which will be noticed later, may ho ablo to do this.

The last fivo epitaphs exhibit these forms:—

   avils kis muvalchl(s).
   avils kis kealch(l)s.
.. avouke lupum avils (m)achs mealchls.*
   avils machs semphalchls† lupu.

---

* In accordance with the other forms, I drop the final k here, which would probably belong to the following word. Such mistakes are not uncommon.

† Thus written in Fabretti's inscriptions, which the other forms shew to be right: in his vocabulary, semphachls.

avils *thuneri muvalchls* lupu.
" ætatis .... obit."

The age of the deceased is obviously given by the words in italics. What then is the meaning of *-alchls* or *lchls*, which is found in all five of these numerals? Or rather, what is the meaning of *-lchl*, for *s* may be the sign of the genitive or plural? In all probability, *-lchl* is "-decim," or "-ginta," or "-genti." But it is not likely to be "-ginta," for *tier-s* and *kiem-z* are "triginta" and "quinqua-ginta." Nor would it be "-decim," for *machs semphalchlı* is shewn by the effigy on the tomb to be the age of an "old man," who was certainly out of his *teens*, unless they were *teens* of *lustres*. *Lchl* would thus appear to be "-genti," = *centum*. Now the Latin *centum* and the Sanskrit *çata* are each 10 × 10, and = *decem-decem-tum* and *daçandaçan-ta*. *Lchl* is probably a similar form, as may be intimated by the repetition of the *l*, and = *lch-lch*, 10 × 10. We have therefore to trace *lch*, "ten."

It is found first in the Lapponic *lokke*, "ten," where we have also the form *lokkad lokke*, "quod dicit *decimum decem*, hoc est *centum*" (Ihre). The Lapponic *lokk-et*, "numerare, legere," shews that the fundamental idea in *lokke*, "ten," is the same as in δέκα, which is connected with δείκω, = *dico*, "λέγω." In fact, *lokke* is "*digit*, number," and is allied to the Lapponic suffix *-lokk*, "omnis, unusquisque," from which we may pass to the Armenian *lok*, "solus, simplex," and to the Tuschi *-loghe* or *-lghe*, which forms ordinals out of cardinals, as in *yethchloghe*, "sixth," from *yethch*, "six," and *qhalghe*, "third," from *qho*, "three."

Lch, "ten," may also be explained from the Lithuanian *-lika,* "-leven, -teen," i. e. "ten," which would = the Polish *lik,* "number." It cannot thus be said that the Etruscan *-lchl,* "-genti," is necessarily of Turanian origin; though, if it were so, it would not be surprising, as the Alpine *lawine,* "avalanche," and *käss,* "glacier," appear to be Turanian words, and the latter = Lapponic *kaisse,* "mons altior, plerumque nive tectus." Yet I think *lchl* is most likely Turanian; for there were, as will be found, Turanian numerals in Etruscan, and the Aryan for "hundred" in Etruscan seems to be *tesnsteis,* a reduplication of *tesns,* "ten," = Armenian *tasn.*

All now comes out easily. *Me-a-lchls* and *muv-a-lchls* both signify "one-hundred" or "one-hundredth;" the Etruscan *me-* and *muv-,* "one," corresponding to the two Armenian forms, *mi* and *mov,* "one," with *me-* in *me-tasan,* "eleven." The connecting vowel *a,* in *me-a-lchls* and *muv-a-lchls,* and in the other similar Etruscan forms, is the same as in Armenian, where we find *mi-a-pet,* "μόν-αρχος;" *mi-a-kin,* "having only one wife;" *char-a-chayl,* "quadruped;" *char-a-kerp,* "quadriform." *Ke-a-lchls* is "five-hundred" or "five-hundredth;" for it will soon be seen that "five" is *ki,* as well as *kiem,* in Etruscan. We have, too, the Armenian *yi-sovn,* "fifty," as well as *hing,* "five;" and we know that *m* is elided in Latin between two vowels, as in *co-arguo,* = *cum-arguo.* Finally, *semph-a-lchls,* if *semph* be right, is "seven-hundred," or "seven-hundredth;" *semph-,* "seven," being = Latin *septem,*

Sanskrit *saptan*, Slavonic *sedmj*, Russian *sem*, Zend *haptan*, Armenian *evthn*, *eóthn*, Greek ἑπτά. The Armenian *evthn*, "seven," would explain the Albanian *yavë* and the Rhæto-Romanco *evna*, "week," just as the Kurdish *ahft*, "seven," explains the Kardish *ahftie*, "week." The present Albanian word for "seven" is *šta(të)*, from which *yavë* could not be derived. The Armenian for "week" is *evthneak* or *eavthneak*.

The Etruscan "-goati" forms may throw some light on another question. The Aryans use three distinct words for "thousand." The Slavonian and Lithuanian terms are like the German *tausend*, as the Armenian *hazar* is like the Sanskrit *sahasra*, and the Celtic *mile* and *mil* are like the Latin *mille*. The Etruscan *mealchl*, "one-hundred," might lead us to explain *mille* as "one-thousand," as if $=mi\text{-}lch \times lch \times lch$ contracted; and it is possible that $\chi i\lambda\text{-}\iota o\iota$ might be "thousand," $= (\lambda)\chi \times \lambda(\chi \times \lambda\chi)$, as *centum* is *(decende)centum*. The forms of *mil* and $\chi i\lambda$- are like the Tuschi *met*, "quot," which appears derived from *me*, "qui," by the addition of *t*, "number," = Lapponio *lokkc*, = Etruscan *lch*, = Polish *lik*. "How many there are"="what a number there are."

Nothing remains for explanation but *machs*, *thunesi*, and *kis*. Now *machs semphalchls*, as is known by the effigy, is the age of an "old man," who might have lived nearly sixty years, or about "seven-hundred months." *Machs* would thus be the genitive or plural of *mach*, "a month," = Sanskrit *más*, "moon," =

Persian *mâh*, = Armenian *mah-ik* (a diminutive in *ik*),
"the crescent moon." The letter-change in the Etruscan *mach*, from the Sanskrit sibilant to the Aric aspirate, should not be overlooked; but in the Armenian *amis*, "month," it is not observed. Finally, as *ril* is "year," and *mach* is "month," *thuncsi* (p. 42) would be "days," or "day's," and is explained by the Armenian *tovnĵean*, which is used as the genitive of *tiv*, "a day," and might be the proper genitive of *tovniğ*, as *teslean* is of *tesil*. Lars (2335 a) would be an infant who only reached the age of a hundred days, while Ramtha (2340), who is described as *puiam*, "filiam," would be a girl of a hundred months old, or in her ninth year when she died. I have not distinguished the two Etruscan characters for *s*, one of which, that in *thuncsi*, is supposed to correspond to the English *sh*, which is nearly the Armenian *ĵ*.

The Etruscan *thuncś(i)* and the Armenian *tovniğ* appear to be composed of the Armenian *tov(oy)*, the genitive of *tiv*, "a day,"—a word which may be allied to *thiv*, gen. *thovoy*, "number, year, epoch,"—and of the Armenian *niś*, gen. *nśi*, i.e. *nëśi*, "sign, mark," = Hebrew *nés*. The Armenian combines *niś* with the pronouns, *ays*, *ayn*, "this, that," in the expressions, *ays niś*, *ayn niś*, "such a one, ὁ δεῖνα;" both being forms similar to the Etruscan *thu-neśi*, "diei," and to what would be a genuine Armenian word, *tov-nëǰi*, with the same signification. And let it be remembered that it is not from the resemblance of the Etruscan *thu-neśi* to the Armenian *tov-nëǰi* that it is interpreted "diei." It is from independent argument, not from similarity of sound, that *leine, lupu, avil, ril, mach,* and *thuneš,* are concluded to mean respectively, "lives," "dies," "age," "year," "month," and "day," the six terms which we find in Latin epitaphs where the age of the deceased is given.

Niebuhr noticed that on two occasions the Etruscans made truce with the Romans, once for *twenty,* and the other time for *forty years;* but yet were again at war with them, and apparently without breaking truce, at the end of *eighteen* and *thirty-six* years respectively. Niebuhr explains this by saying that the Etruscan year would have contained only *ten months.* No doubt the explanation is correct, and the truces would have been made for *two-hundred* and *four-hundred months.* This shews how the Etruscans were in the habit of reckoning by periods of *one-hundred months,* each of which periods would have been a kind of double lustre, just as the Latin has *bilustris* for a period of ten years. Of course such periods could only have been used in epitaphs when the age of the deceased happened to be nearly bilustral; and this may explain why, in the case of two members of one family (*ante,* p. 37, cpit. 2070, 2071), the age of one of them is defined by the words, *avils kiemzathrms lupu,* and that of the other by the words, *avils machs semphalchls lupu.* Larth Churchles lived *fifty-three years, ril* being understood; and Arnth Churkles *seven-hundred months,* or about *fifty-eight years.* But perhaps *one-hundred months = eight years.**

---

* An Etruscan week was *eight days* (Niebuhr).

Kis may be explained in two different manners. When *kis muvalchls* and *kis kealchls* are compared with *machs mealchls* and *machs semphalchls* (ante, p. 41), it might be inferred that *kis* = *machs*, and therefore that *ki* means "month." If so, we have another Turanian word; for "moon, month," is *ku* in Esthonian, and *kuu* in Fin; while in Georgian "moon, month," is *thve*, and in Tuschi "white" is *kui*: all terms probably akin ultimately to the Sanskrit *çve(ta)*, "*whi(te)*."* Otherwise, as there is no equivalent for *lupu*, "dies," or *avenke lupum*, "leaves a corpse," in the two epitaphs which contain *kis* (p. 41), that word might be explained from the Armenian *géś*, gen. *giśi*, "a corpse;" and *machs*, "months," would be understood, like *ril*, "years," elsewhere. At any rate, *kisum* would be rendered "*νεκρόν*" in 2340 (ante, p. 37), where it is in apposition to *Ramthn.* The beginning of that epitaph would mean: *Ramtham Matulnæ prolem, Marci Matulnæ filiam, Amycus a Sethre Cæsennia νεκρὸν sepelit*. So, too, in the first line of another epitaph (Fabretti 2339) we read:—

Larth Keisinis Velus klan *kizi zilachnke*—
where *kizi zilachnke* would be rendered "dies (and) is buried," or " (being) dead is buried," or "is buried with the dead;" according as we make *kizi* an Armenian verb like *lini* (ante, p. 29), or a noun like *outi*, "a way," or a noun like *géś*, "a corpse." Very probably, *kis* and *kisum* are unconnected in sense.

---

* Mouna Kea in Hawaii is the "*White Mountain.*" It is the Mont Blanc of the Sandwich Islands.

I now turn to notice the doubtful inscription, *avils sesphs lupuke*, where the *sesphs* of the inscription is given as *semphs* in Fabretti's vocabulary, and there interpreted "seventy," after the analogy of *semph*, "seven," in that form which he gives as *semph-alchls* in his inscriptions, and as *semph-achls* in his vocabulary. There are thus, in Fabretti, three to one in favour of *semph*, "seven," as against *sesph*, which would have to be referred to the Basque *zazpi*, "seven." Now, as *tiers* would be "thirty," *semphs* or *sesphs* would rightly be "seventy," if *semph* or *sesph* be "seven." But there is one objection to the interpretation. The epitaph, *avils sesphs lupuke* or *avils semphs lupuke*, is annexed to the figure of a young man (*giovane*), which would seem from the description of the tomb to represent the deceased, though it may not do so. If it does, as the Etruscan *ph* and *th* nearly resemble each other, the true reading might possibly be *sesths* or *semths* (for *semphths*), "sixteen" or "seventeen." In this case, *-ths* would = Welsh *-theg*, Sanskrit *-daçan*, Armenian *-tasan*; the final *-an* being dropped in *-ths*, just as in the change from the Armenian *-sovn* or *-san*, "-ginta," to the Etruscan *-s*. On the whole, I should think Fabretti's vocabulary and interpretation most likely to be right as to this doubtful word, and that we ought to read *semphs*, "seventy," rather than anything else. But it is not a word that can be much relied on.*

---

* The Etruscan *m* and *s* (*sh*) are liable to be confounded. In the same epitaph, Arnthialum should probably be Arnthialus.

The Porugian Inscription, which appears to be a conveyance of land for a burying-ground, may help us to arrive at some other Etruscan numerals. We find there, in two different parts:—
......*chiemfu*sle.........
and also—   ....sleleth*karu*
            *tezanfus*leri *tesusteis*
            rasnes..................
As *chiem* seems probably = *kiem*, "five," *karutezan* may be a number; and if so, would apparently be "fourteen," = Sanskrit *caturdaçan*, = Armenian *corechtasan*: but in *chara*-sovn, "forty," the Armenian approaches more nearly to the first part of *karu*-tezan. The second extract above concludes with—
            tesnsteis
            rasnes
and we have besides—*tesns* eka velthinathurasth
            aurabelu*tesncrusne*kei
            tesnsteis rasneschimthsp
Here *rasne* would not improbably be the Persian *rasan*, Armenian *arasan*, "a cord," Sanskrit *rasand*, "a girdle," and might mean "fathom." Cf. σχοῖνος ; also German *klafter*, "cord, fathom," *faden*, "thread, fathom." *Fuslo* may have been some larger measure than *rasne*. As we may possibly have *sesths*, "sixteen," elsewhere, *chimths* might be "fifteen ;" though this seems inconsistent with *karutezan*, "fourteen," and is open to other objections. But there would be less reason for doubting that *tesne* is "ten," = Armenian *tasn*,= Sanskrit and Zend *daçan*; and if it be, then

£

tesnsteis would probably be "ten tens," or "a hundred;" a formation like *lchl*, excepting that *tesns-*, "tens," has the sign of the plural. The Armenian *tasn* is declined, the genitive being *tasin*, and the instrumental *tasamb*. The Sanskrit *çata*, "hundred," would be formed from *daça(n)-daça(n)-ta* by a process very different from that employed in the formation of *tesnsteis*. The Armenian for "a hundred" is *harivr*, which is an entirely different word.

Kiem, sas, semph, and *tesne,* have been interpreted "five," "six," "seven," and "ten," by others before myself, as may be seen in Fabretti's index. I now come to something more remarkable than the existence of Aryan numerals in Etruscan; a fact which would have been expected in a language that is plainly Aryan. *There are numerals in Etruscan which are not Aryan,* as *lchls* has perhaps intimated already. This important discovery connects itself with what I said in my first chapter. I there noticed that there were in ancient times *Iberians, Ligyes,* and *Tuscans,* not only along the Mediterranean from Gibraltar to the Tiber, but likewise all three in the Caucasian regions: also that there are now *Toscans* in Albania, and *Tuschi* in the Caucasus; and that the Tuschi word *law*, "snow," explains the *lawine* of the Alps. It appears too from Livy (x. 4) that there was a difference between the town and country speech in Etruria. Now on a pair of Etruscan dice (Fabretti, 2552) the first six numbers are given in words: and by comparing the relative positions of these words with the relative positions, on a quantity of other ancient dice, of the same numbers expressed by points, Campanari has determined their value to be as follows:—

I	II	III	IV	V	VI.
mach	*thu*	*zal*	*huth*	*ki*	*sa.**

Here *mach* is Aryan, and may be compared with the Armenian *miak*, "unique, one." *Thu* and *sa* are Aryan, though not exclusively, as they are like the Circassian *tu* and the Basque *sei*. The Irish for "six" is *sé*. *Zal*, "three," is not Aryan. *Huth* is not Aryan,

---

* I do not know whether any exceptions will be taken to my interpretations of *machs*, *kis*, and *thunesi* (*ante*, p. 41), because *mach*, *ki*, and *thu* are here found to be Etruscan numerals. But, if *machs* and *kis* be there interpreted as "first" and "fifth," we should then have to understand *ril*, "year," and therefore to interpret *mealchls* and *muvalchls* as "tenth," *kealchls* as "fiftieth," and *semphalchls* as "seventieth." This seems to me improbable: and even if it were allowable to interpret *muvalchls* as "tenth," what are we to make of *thunesi* in *avils thunesi muvalchls lupu*, "œtatis (anni for anno)......(et) decimi obit?" *Thunesi* ought to be the genitive of a number, as well as *machs* and *kis*, and would therefore have to signify "eight" or "nine," as all the other numeral places are occupied. Now *thu* is "two" in Etruscan, and there are languages, of which the Hungarian is one, where "eight" = 4 × 2; so that *thu-nesi* or *thu-nes* might be "eight," if *nesi* or *nes* were "four"; and "four" is *négy* in Hungarian, and *nel* in Ostiak, two Finnish dialects. Indeed, "eight" in Ostiak is *nida*, which would = *nei-da*, 4 × 2. It is thus possible for *thu-nesi* to be "eight." But, if *muva-lchl-s* be "ten," the second *l* would be non-radical, as *lch*, according to analogy, would mean "ten" by itself. Yet this might not be impossible, as the *t* termination in the Classical, Zend, and Sanskrit "-ginta" and "-genti" forms is non-radical too, and the *t* termination of the Sanskrit participle becomes, as will appear later, an *l* termination in Armenian and Etruscan. Or lch-l might be "ten-*h*," as qha-*lghe* is "thir-d" in Tuschi (*ante*, p. 42).

and both *huth* and *ki* seem Caucasian. This may appear by comparing these six Etruscan numerals with the same numerals in Circassian, Tuschi, Georgian, and Lazic:—

	I	II	III	IV	V	VI.
Circassian	.se	tu	śi	ptľe	ťchu	chi.
Tuschi	...zha	śi	qho	dhew	phchi	yethch.
Georgian	...erthi	ori	sami	othkhi	khuthi	ckhvsi.
Lazio	......ar	zur	ǵum	otkh	khut	aś.
Etruscan	...mach	thu	zal	huth	ki	sa.

In *th-khu-meti*, "fifteen," the Georgian *khuthi*, "five," is contracted to *khu*.* The Etruscan *ki*, "five," might be obtained from the Georgian *kh(uth)i*, or the Tuschi *(ph)chi;* or nearly from the Circassian *(ť)chu;* or from the Lesgi *chewa* and *yku*, which mean "five" in two different dialects; or from the Abkhasian *chu(ba)*, "five," where *ba* is a suffix for all numerals from two to ten, so that *chu* would be the number "five." The Etruscan *huth*, "four," would probably not be the *oth* of the Georgian *othkhi*, "four," but would be related to the Georgian *khuthi*, "five," and the Lazic *khut*, nearly as the Georgian *o-thkhi*, "four," and the Tuschi *ye-thch*, "six," are to the Circassian *ťchu*, "five." For the Georgian *-thkhi* in *o-thkhi*, and the Tuschi *-thch* in *ye-thch*, are both apparently = Circassian *ťchu*, "five," while the Tuschi *ye* in *ye-thch*, and the Georgian *o* in *o-thkhi*, may both be explained from the Ossetic *yu, yeu,* or *ycue*, "one." That is to

---

* *Th-* is "ten," and *-meti* is like the Ostiak ordinal sign *-met*.

say, the Georgian *o-thkhi*, "four," is "one *from* five," IV; and the Tuschi *ye-thch*, "six," is "one *to* five," VI. So, in the Georgian *ekh-vsi*, "six," *-vsi* would probably = Fin *wiisi*, "five," while *ekh-* is "one," = Sanskrit *eka*, = Persian *yak*, = Abkhasian *aku*, = Hungarian *egy*, = Fin *yk*, which becomes *yh-* in *yh-deksa*, "nino," i. o. "one from ten," IX. If now the *ekh-*, "one," of the Georgian *ekh-vsi*, "six," be prefixed to the Georgian *khuthi*, "five," we could obtain for "one *from* five," IV, the form *ekh-khuthi*, which might be changed, by incorporation and contraction, into the Etruscan *huth*, "four," in which a χ, implying "one," is lost at the beginning of the word, as it would really be also in the Etruscan *sa*, "six," as well as in the Sanskrit *śaś*. The following tabular view may present the argument more clearly:—

Etruscan ......(χ)——*sa*,   VI (= *one + five*).
Abkhasian ...   *śva*,   X (= *fives*).
Ossetic.........*ach* — *sāz*, VI (= *one + five**).
Zend ....*kh*——*svas*, VI.
Sanskrit ... { (χ)——*śaś*, VI.
              { *eka*, ... I.
Abkhasian ...*aka*, ... I.
Ossetic...... { *yu*, ... I.
              { *yeu*, ... I.
Circassian ...   *t'chu*,   V.
Tuschi ....*ye*——*thch*, VI.

---

* That *sāz*, etc., probably = "five," will be shewn in the last chapter. The true value is seen in the Basjui *sarpi*, "seven," where *·pi* = *bi*, "two."

Georgian ...	{	0 —— thkhi,	iv.
		. khuthi,	v.
Lazic	{	0 —— tkh,	iv.
		khut,	v.
Etruscan ...	{	(χ)——huth,	iv.
		ki,	v.
Lesgi		chewa,	v.
Circassian ...(χ)——		chi,	vi.
Tuschi.........		phchi,*	v.
Abkhasian ...(χ)——		phśi,	iv.
Circassian ...		pśo,	x (= fives).

It will be perceived from the forms at the head of this table how a guttural aspirate is lost before *s*. But such an aspirate would be still more likely to be lost when it preceded another aspirate, as in that case the fusion of the two aspirates into one would be almost sure to take place. And so, by the loss of the prefixed aspirate implying I, the Etruscan *huth*, iv, may = the Georgian *khuthi* and the Lazic *khut*, v, nearly as the Abkhasian *phśi*, iv, = Tuschi *phchi*, v, and as the Circassian *chi*, vi, = Etruscan *ki*, v. As *Octavius* is written *Uhtave* in Etruscan, the Etruscan *h* would be guttural, like the Hebrew *cheth* which it represents. The explanation of the Etruscan *zal*, "three," must be reserved to the fifth chapter, where the subject of numerals can be more fully discussed: at present I can only exhibit it in connexion with some other numerals for "three," to which it appears wholly or partially allied :—

---

* Cf. Georgian *phekhi*, "foot."

Finnish	Fin ....ko-lmi		
	Syrianic ......kn-jm*		
Caucasian	Lazic ....ju-m	"three," =	
	Mingrelian ...su-mi	"2 from 5,"	
	Georgian ......sa-mi	IIV.	
	Etruscan ......za-l		
	Javaneso ......la-lu		

Another representative of "five," *l* or *l-m*, is introduced here, and may also be found in the Circassian *pt-l'e*, IV, and *b'le*, VII.† Such terms for "five," as will be shewn in the sequel, are all different words for "hand" or "foot" : the Cornish *lau*, the Gaelic *làmh*, the Turkish *él*, and the Malay *lima*, all signify "hand." It is rather strange that the Etruscans should have used two languages for the numbers on their dice: but we do something of the same kind in England, as we usually employ French names for the numbers on dice, but sometimes English; while in the case of cards we begin with French, but soon pass into English. If the language of the Rasenæ be represented by Anglo-French, and that of the Pelasgians by English, then the six numbers on the Etruscan dice would be: *ace, deuce* (or *two*), *three, four, five, six*. *Sa* might be *nice*, but I think it more likely to be *six*, as *sas* would be the Etruscan representative of *sice*. Yet, as *sa* is

---

* In speaking, we drop *l* before *m* in *holm*, and in *balm, calm, psalm*: but we retain it in *elm, helm,* and *whelm*, and also in *film*.

† In Basque, *bat* is I, *bi* is II, and *lau* is IV, perhaps rightly V. If so, the two Circassian forms are easily explained from the Basque, as "one from five," and "two to five."

"six," *sas* might be "sixty" in Etruscan, if we had not *avils tiers sas* as well as *avils sas*. But how would the Etruscans have expressed "sixty," which, if *sas* were "six," ought according to analogy to be *sas-s* or *sas-z*? The Armenian gets over the difficulty by changing *z* into *th*. Thus "six" is *wez*; "sixteen," *westasan*; and "sixty," *wathsovn*.

I have spoken of the Etruscan numerals, *zal*, *huth*, *ki*, and *sa*, as being *Pelasgian*. Now that there were Pelasgians in Etruria is so commonly known that one quotation will suffice. The writer who is called Scymnus Chius says:—

Μετὰ τὴν Λιγυστικὴν Πελασγοὶ δ' εἰσὶν, οἱ
Πρότερον κατοικήσαντες ἐκ τῆς Ἑλλάδος,
Κοινὴν δὲ Τυρρηνοῖσι χώραν νεμόμενοι.

To what element in the population of Etruria, unless to the Pelasgians, can we attribute the numerals in question? We know the Umbrian language to be an Aryan dialect resembling the Latin, and we meet continually with *tre* and *tref*, "three," in the Eugubine Tables. The Tyrrhenians, again, as distinguished above from the Pelasgians, are there derived, according to the common tradition, from Lydia, and would have spoken that Aryan language of the Armenian type which we have found predominant in Etruria. The conclusion seems almost inevitable. We learn from Herodotus that the Pelasgians whom he knew spoke a *barbarous* dialect. It would now appear that it was not even Aryan; although, if the numerals in question be considered as Caucasian, and the origin of the

Etruscans from Armenia he admitted, it might be urged as possible that the Etruscans borrowed them when there from the Caucasians, who would have possessed Armenia before the Aryans came thither out of Media. I should, however, for my own part, entirely reject such a solution, especially as the numerals are not the only indication of the presence of Caucasians in the South of Europe.

The following list will comprise such numerals as have been detected in Etrusean :—

    I. *mach, me-, muo-*
    II. *thu*
    III. *zal, thr-*
    IV. *huth, kar-* (?)
    V. *ki, ke-, kiem-, chiem* (?)
    VI. *sa, sas*
    VII. *se(m)ph*
    X. *tesno*
    XIV. *karutezan* (?)
    XV. *chimths* (?)
    XXX. *ti(e)rs.*
    L. *kiemz-*
    LIII. *kiemzathr-*
    LXX. *se(m)phs* (?)
    C. *tesnstein, mealchl, muvalchl*
    D. *koalchl*
    DCC. *se(m)phalchl*

We see here an Aryan language which contains some Turanian words, as *dozen* and *century* are contained in the English language. The explanation has just been suggested. The *Rasenæ*, or Tyrrhenians of Etruria, were Aryans of the Thracian stock, while the *Tuscans*, who were the *Pelasgians* or "Aborigines" (*ante*, p. 11) of the country, were Turanians, and probably Caucasians. It seems likely, however, that the blood of the Etruscans, and of the Thracians in general, was more Turanian than their language, as the primitive Caucasian population on which they intruded would have been incorporated with them into one people. The language of the Etruscan nobles may have been at first Thracian, with some Caucasian accretions acquired on the way from Armenia to Etruria, while the language of the *Tuscan* commonalty may have been Caucasian, perhaps with a little Umbrian also. The languages would probably in time have coalesced, as Anglo-Saxon, Danish, and Norman-French did into English; but in Etruria it was the language of the aristocracy which prevailed. The Etruscan language is Thracian, while the English is German.*

---

* Mr. Fergusson has inferred, on architectural and other grounds distinct from language, the Turanian character of the Pelasgians and Etruscans. I must come over to his opinion, as far as the Pelasgians are concerned. When I extended the Caucasians into Europe nine years ago, it was not among them, but among the Thracians, that I was inclined to include the Pelasgians. One result of the Thracian invasion of Europe by the Hellespont and the Bosphorus would probably have been a concentration of Pelasgians in Greece. To this predominant Pelasgian or Caucasian element in their blood the Greeks may have been greatly indebted for their beauty of form: nor would that form have undergone much alteration from what it was at first, if the Thracian element in the Greek population consisted principally of maritime settlers, *Leleges*, from Asia Minor, and the Italian element of

In the epitaphs which gave us the Etruscan numerals, we met with *klan, puiam,* and *sech,* words all indicating parentage or descent. *Klan,* which corresponds to *natus* in a bilingual inscription, seems connected with the Gaelic *clann,* "offspring, descendants"; the Welsh *plan,* "a scion," and *plant,* "a son;" the Latin *planta;* and the Greek κλάς, κλάδος, κλών, κλάω, φλάω, τλάω; words which may be allied to the Armenian *khl-el;* "to tear away, to root up (*déplanter*)," as *glan,* the Armenian for "cylinder," is derived from *gl-el,* "to roll." But another interpretation is given by K. O. Müller (*Die Etrusker,* vol. i, p. 446). He compares the two inscriptions on the same monument:

La. Venete La. Lethinl* etera
So. Veneto Ln. Lethial *klan*

and observes: "If *etera* be taken to mean 'other, second,' *klan* must be 'first, firstborn.'" *Etera* is thus compared with the Greek ἕτερος, = Armenian *ōtar*. Dr. Donaldson argues in the same manner (*Varronianus,* p.

---

maritime settlers, *Hellenes,* from Messapia and its neighbourhood. In blood, though not in language, the Greeks and Lycians may have been very nearly allied, like the people of Cornwall and Brittany. Gauls have become French in like manner.

Of the Etruscan words mentioned by ancient writers, one is apparently Turanian. This word is *damnus,* "*Ixros,*" which seems allied to the Lapponic *támp,* "equus," the Fin *tamma,* "equa," the Armenian *sambik,* "equa, *jument,*" the Basque *samaria,* "jumentum vectorium, *caballería,*" the Albanian *samaros,* "jumentum," the Pehlvi *djemna,* "camel," and the Mantschu *temen,* "camel." The Armenian has taken up some Turanian words.

* *Lethe,* a man's name, and *Lethi,* a woman's name, are in Fabretti (1039).

171): "If then *etera* means, as is most probable, the second of a family, *klan* must mean the *first* or *head* of the family." This might bring us to the Armenian *glovkh* (= Polish *głowa*), "head, summit, the first rank;" *glkhan zovkn*, "chub" (lit. "head-fish"); *glkhani*, "the chief persons in a city, the nobility." As there exists *rain* by the side of *regen*, and *wain* by the side of *waggon* and *wayen*, the aspirate *kh* might be dropped in *glkhan*.

Another group of words is presented by the following epitaphs in Lanzi:—

191. mi Kalairu *fuius*
315. Lth. Marikane *via*
310. Larthi Vetus Klaukes *puia*
311. Arnth Vipis Scrturis *puiak*....
123. Anes Kaes *puil* (t)hui....

The Latin *filius* and the Greek *υἱός* would be allied to these terms, and also the Gaelic *fuil* "blood, family, tribe, kindred." In Finnish dialects we find the Hungarian *fiú*, "son," the Syrianic *pi*, "son," and the Esthonian *poia*, "son." The Wallachian is very complete here; for it gives us *pulu*, "what is young," *filu*, "son," *fia*, "daughter," and *fiika*, "*θυγάτριον, töchterlein.*" I find no such words in Armenian. The next expression appears to be both Finnish and Armenian:

63. Larthia Kaia Huzetnas Arnthalisa Kafatl *sak*
37. Titi Velimnias Akril *sek*
471. Ramthn Matulnei *sech*....

Lapponic *sakko*, "proles." Armenian *zag-il*, "to be born or derived;" *zag-el*, "to produce young;" *zag*, "a young bird (νεοσσός)," = Albanian zok. The Armenian *zag* and the Albanian *zok* mean also "a small bird," and are both employed to render "sparrow" (Luke x, 6).

The next expressions are of peculiar interest on account of the monuments where they are found, as they occur in the celebrated "valley of tombs" at Castel d'Asso, as well as at Norchia and Toscanella, and elsewhere. But their philological importance is of a still higher character, as they seem to dispose of the claims of the Sanskrit to include the Etruscan in its own peculiar division of the Aryan languages, while the claims of the Armenian stand the test, and are confirmed by the Etruscan forms. One of these forms is *eka suthi* (accompanied by a proper name in the nominative); an expression which Migliarini conjectures to mean "hic situs est," or "questa è la tomba," and which must, indeed, have some similar signification. The other form is *eka suthi nesl*; and one example of it is *eka suthi nesl Tetnie*, which I should render, "here is buried the dead Titinia, *hic conditur mortua* (necata) *Titinia*;" considering *eka suthi nesl* to be now represented in Armenian by *ahá sovzani nekheal*, "ecce seso condit putrefactus," which does not, however, exhibit the affinity which the Armenian bears to the Etruscan so clearly as it may be brought out by further consideration.

The letter-changes in different Aryan languages should be noticed here. Now we have in the first place—Sanskrit *hrid* = English *heart* = German *herz*

= Greek καρδ- = Latin cord- = Gaelic cridhe = Welsh craidd = Armenian sirt = Lithuanian szird- = Polish serce ; and in the next place—Sanskrit çvan = English hound = German hund = Greek κυν- = Latin can- = Gaelic cu = Welsh ci = Armenian šovn = Lithuanian szun-.* From this it may be seen that, while German languages retain the Sanskrit h, and convert the Sanskrit ç into h, and while Celtic and Classical languages convert both into k, = c, (and sometimes into g), Thracian and Sarmatian languages represent both by sibilants. Now let us apply this principle to deal with the roots of—

   suth-i nes-l
   "cond-itnr nec-atns."

If these two Etruscan words are rightly translated into Latin (supposing necatus = mortuus), then the following comparisons will show, by the aid of the letter-changes, that the roots of the Etruscan and Latin are the same in both words, and that the Etruscan is like the Armenian in all respects. For we should have :—

Sanskrit { hud, " concervare, submergi."   Cf. hṛid
    { hund, " concervare."
{ Welsh ...cudd-, " to hide."   craidd
{ Latin ...cond-, " to hide, to bury."   cord-
{ Lithuanian .szut-, " acervus."   szird-
{ Armenian . sovz-, " to hide, to submerge."   sirt
{ Etruscan .. suth-, " to bury."

---

* Bötticher defines the Aric, or Thracian and Persian languages, as differing from Indian, German, and Latin, by using h for s, s for h, and s for ç.

Sanskrit. *naç*, "perire, mori."   Cf. *daç*-an, "ten."
{ Latin . *nec*-, "kill."   *dec*-em.
{ Greek. *νεκ*-, " dio."   δέκ-α.
{ Armenian. *naš*, " a coffin."   *tas*-n.
{ Etruscan . *nes*, " die."   *tes*-ne.
Anglo-Saxon. *nâ, nê*, "corpse."   *ty*-n, "*zeh*-n."

Similar letter-changes occur in the Sanskrit *spaç*, "perficere," = Armenian *spas*, "function, service," *spas*-el, "to serve, to observe, to watch (*épier*)", = Latin *spec*-, = German *späh*-en, = English *spy*. The Armenian *nekh*-, "putrescere," found above in *nekh-eal*, "putrefactus," would not represent the Sanskrit *naç*, "mori," so much as the cognate Sanskrit *nakk*, "necare, destruere." There is a corresponding pair of forms in the Armenian *doustr* and *dokht*, "daughter," = Sanskrit *duhitṛi*, Zend *dughdar*, Persian *dokhter*, *dokht*, Lithuanian *dukte*, Slavonic *dūšti*. The termination of the Etruscan *nes-l*, = Latin *nec-atus*, is found in the Armenian *nekh-eal*. The Slavonic resembles the Armenian in having the Sanskrit and Latin *t* of the preterite participle converted into the weaker *l*; but the Lithuanian retains the *t* unchanged. Some Indian dialects exhibit *l* in the place of *t*, like the Armenian and Slavonic. In the preterite participle of the Sanskrit *naç*, the *ç* becomes *š*; and *našṭa*, "perditus," = Etruscan *nesl*, "mortuus," which resembles closely in *form* the Slavonic *nes-l'*, "having borne."

We have considered the roots of the Etruscan *suth-i nes-l*, as well as the form of *nes-l*, and have found them all throe in the Armenian language. It only remains to notice the form of *suth-i,* "conditur." Now the general characteristic of the Armenian passive is *i*, which is equivalent to that of the Sanskrit passive, *ya*. Thus, in Armenian, "he loves" is *sir-é*, while "he is loved" is *sir-i,* which is just the form of *suth-i.* The corresponding Sanskrit form would be *-yate;* the Etruscan and Armenian converting the Sanskrit *ya* into *i*, and dropping the *t* of the third person, with the vowel that follows it. In the aorist, however, the Armenian employs the *a*, not the *y(i)* of the Sanskrit *ya*, to form the passive: thus *sirez̈-i* is "I loved," and *sirez̈-ay* is "I was loved." Compare $\tau i\theta\eta\mu$-ι and $\tau i\theta\epsilon\mu$-$\alpha\iota$, $\tau\upsilon\pi\tau\epsilon(\tau)$-$\iota$ and $\tau\upsilon\pi\tau\epsilon\tau$-$\alpha\iota$.*

The Rhæto-Romance *talipp*, "locust," = Sanskrit *çalabha,* "locust," = Armenian *satap*, "gliding, quick," implies that the ancient Rhætian was like the Armenian and Etruscan in one of its letter-changes. The Greek and Latin give *kel-* for the Sanskrit *çal,* "run." The Rhæto-Romance *as-oula,* "kid" (*ante,* p. 7), if

---

* The characteristic of the Latin passive, *r*, is Celtic. Thus we find in Zeuss (*Grammatica Celtica*) these Irish forms:—*predch-idir*, "predic-atur"—*consuidig-ther*, "compon-itur"—*tuc-atar*, "intellig-untur"—*tomn-ib-ther*, "cogit-ab-itur"—and *prom-f-idir,* "prob-ab-itor." In the last two examples, the characteristic *b* of the Latin future appears also, as again in the Irish car-*ub,* "am abo," and the rest of the persons: cair-*fe,* cair-*fed,* car-*fam,* cair-*fid,* car-*fat.* In the Welsh par-*ossei,* "effecerit," and agysg-*ossei,* "dormiverit," we meet with forms similar to am-*dssel:* and in *chlyw-yssynt,* "aud-*ivissent,* aud-*issent,*" the Latin form with the root of κλύ-ω, in-*cly-tus,* and *cli-ens.* The oldest Celtic writings, from which forms like these are taken, reach back about as far as 800 A.D.

allied to *aiy-* and the Armenian *ayž*, would mark a similar peculiarity.

If the Etruscan *suth-* = Sanskrit *hud*, "coacervare, submergi," = Armenian *sovz-*, "hide, submerge," then the Aryan family to which the Etruscan belongs would not be Sanskrit, but Armenian, as it is between these two families that our choice would lie. Yet, as the question seems to be reduced to this point, it may be as well to notice another distinction between the Sanskrit on one side, and the Armenian and the Etruscan on the other. The Sanskrit names for a town are *pura, nagara,* and *pattana,* the *-poor, -nagore,* and *-patam* of our present India. But Etruria exhibits none of these names (though *pattana* resembles the Venetian *Patavium*), while the corresponding Armenian term, *sén,* gen. *sini,* does appear there, and may indeed serve to trace the Etruscan route from the supposed "Primeval Country" of the Aryans at the sources of the Oxus and the Jaxartes, up to the Po and the Tiber. The following names, which are all taken from one author, Ptolemy, may be sufficient to exemplify this; and it will be observed that even the Armenian vowel-change from *sén,* "village, habitation," to its genitive *sini,* and *sin-el,* "to build," is not without significance:—

Among "the mountain-towns of the Sogdians along the Jaxartes" is—

Χολβη-σίνα*..................Sogdiana.

---

* Ptolemy mentions two Armenian towns called Χολούα, and another called Χολου-άτα. Cf. Armenian *holow,* "a round."

F

Σίνα or Σήνα .... Margiana.
Σινάκα* .... Hyrcania.
Σαναίς .... Media.
Σάνα }
Σινίς } .... Armenia.
Σανίς .... Phrygia.
'Οπί-σινα or 'Οπί-σηνα† ...... Thrace.
Σενία .... Illyria.
Και-σαίνα‡ .... Cisalpine Gaul.
Σαίνα§ }
Ούολ-σίνιον } .... Etruria.

Fel-*sina*, the Etruscan name of Bononia (Bologna), and Sar-*sina*, may be added from other authorities. The Lithuanian here touches the Thracian again ; for in Lithuanian *sĕna* means " wall," and *sēnys*, " building." The root is also used in Georgian, and Sinope looks as if it were the Georgian *senoba*, "building." Cf. *ifipfa* (*ante*, p. 21).

Pliny writes, (*H. N.*, vi. 31): " Oritur (Tigris) in regione Armeniæ majoris, fonte conspicuo in planitie. Loco nomen *Elegosine* est." This is a compound name like *Volsinium, Felsina*, and *Sarsina*. The ancients mention two places in Armenia called *Elegia*, and one in Noricum called *Elegium*. Pliny writes again (xvi. 66): " Est et obliqua *arundo* ... vocatur a quibusdam *elegia*." One could wish that he had named

---

* Armenian diminutives are formed in -*ak*.
† Compare *ὀπ*- with the Armenian *oph*, " trench."
‡ Cf. Armenian *kay*, = Sanskrit *kâya*, " domus."
§ *Sena*, now *Siena*.

these *quidam*, for *elegia* would be the Armenian *ełegn*, "a reed," which appears again in the Phrygian ἔλυμος, "αὐλός,"* as well as in the Greek ἔλεγος, a word probably borrowed by the Ionians from the Lydians. It is said on the Arundel Marble: "Τάγνις ὁ Φρὺξ αὐλοὺς πρῶτος ηὗρεν; and by Pausanias (x. 7): Ἐλεγεῖα καὶ θρῆνοι προσᾳδόμενα τοῖς αὐλοῖς.

One use that the Armenians made of reeds was, according to Xenophon, to suck up beer or barley-wine through them. This practice the Armenians had in common with the Phrygians and Thracians; a fact mentioned in his *History of Greece* by Mr. Grote, who adds, with a just appreciation of national relationship: "The similarity of Armenian customs to those of the Thracians and Phrygians is not surprising." *Næniæ*, like ἐλεγεῖα, were sung to the flute, which is called in Armenian *ełegnaphoł*, "reed-trumpet." Thus Cicero says (*De Leg.*, ii, 24): "Cantus ad *tibicinem*, cui nomen *næniæ*." Compare νηνίατον or νινίατος, "Φρύγιον μέλος," on which word Bötticher observes: "*Nænia* Romanorum in mentem venit, et radix *nu*, 'laudare.'" This Sanskrit root is found in the Armenian *nov-ag*, "a song," and *nov-al*, "to mew"; while *νη-* or *næ-* may be referred to the Persian *nay*, "flute," = Sanskrit *naḍa*, "arundinis species," = Armenian *neł*, "sagitta," i. e. "calamus." Thus *nænia* seems the *nay-nu*, "flute-song," just like ἔλεγος. The Armenian word for "lute," *win*, is the Sanskrit *vīṇā*, "lute";

---

* Bötticher's *Arica*, p. 34.

and the Armenian *chnar*, "lyre," is obviously the Greek κινύρα and the Hebrew *kinnor*. We may see by these instances what the comparison of languages has exhibited all along from the first (*ante*, p. 7), how Armenia was connected with India on one side, and still more closely with Asia Minor, Thrace, and Italy, on the other.

In addition to *Lorium* (*ante*, p. 29), and *Sena*, *Felsina*, and *Volsinium*, or *Volsinii*, other Etruscan names of towns may be explained from the Armenian:— *Veii*, ἐφ' ὑψηλοῦ σκοπέλου, from *veh*, "high"—*Volci*, or Ὄλκιον, from *oïtkh*, "a ravine"—*Hasta*, from *hast*, "strong"—*Blera*, from *blovr*, "a hill," and *blrak*, "a hillock"—*Aharna*, from *akarn*, "a castle"—and *Nepete*, from Mount *Npat* (Niphates), and *npatak*, "object, mark." Compare σκοπιά and σκόπελος.

I return from this rather long digression to complete the examination of Etruscan sepulchral forms of expression.

An Etruscan word for "tomb" appears to be *tular*. *Tularu* is found in the Perugian Inscription, and Lanzi supplies these four epitaphs :—

457. *tulat* Rasnal
458. *tular* Hilar ....
460. *tular* Svuriu Au. Papsinasl ....
461. Tetrnter*tular*.

Tular may be interpreted "*tumulus*," and thus connected with the Greek τύλη, τύλαρος, and the Gaelic *tulu*, "hillock"; or else be explained from the Armenian *that*, "tellus," *thatel*, "to bury," *thatar*, "an earthen vessel." Lanzi supposed *tular* = τὸ ollarium. No Etruscan phrase has yet been noticed which expresses the sentiment of the Greek μνείας χάριν or μνήμης ἕνεκεν, or of our English "in memory of." But I believe that we have one in the following epitaphs in Lanzi :—

76. Thutnei *thui*
80. Laris Vete *thui*
313. *Thui* Larth Petrni Larthalisa.

Thui might be interpreted "nominatur, memoratur," by the aid of these Armenian analogies :—

thiv (gen. *thovoy*), "numerus."
thovel, "numerare."
thové, "numerat."
thovi, "numeratur."
thovich (plural form of *thovi*), "sententia."

The next epitaph (Lanzi, No. 86) would thus imply that the person named *is commemorated*, and *lived* (i. e. is dead) :—

Larth Vete Arnthalisa *thui*. Larth Vete *line*.*

Thovi, it will be seen, being implied in *thovich*, is both a noun and a verb in Armenian; and in like manner the Etruscan *suthi* would probably signify not only "is buried," but also "grave, tomb." For the following inscription is given by Lanzi (vol. ii, p. 562):—

mi suthi Larthial Muthikus.

"I (am) the tomb of Muthious the son of Lartia."†

---

* Why should the Latin line, "unge," be considered a probable explanation of this Etruscan line?

† We know from Herodotus that the Lydian *Myrsil(us)* meant "the son of *Myrs(us)*."

It might, however, signify: "Muthicas the son of Lartia is haried in me." The stone containing this inscription was discovered at Busca, between Cuneo and Saluzzo, in the country of the ancient Vagienni; a remarkable locality for an Etruscan epitaph, though it might imply no more than a Greek inscription would do at Rome, or an English epitaph in a French or German cemetery.

In addition to the numerals, the Etruscan epitaphs will have furnished us with the following forms, which I collect together here. If the interpretations were undoubtedly true, the Etruscan question might probably be considered at an end. Where the Etruscan forms are accompanied by a number, it is represented by N. The proper name has to be supplied.

avil N
avils N } "ætatis N."

ril N, "annos N," or "anno N."

line, "vivebat."

avil ril N, "anno ætatis N."

ril leine N
ril N leine } "vivit annos N."

lupu, "obit."

lupu avils N
avils N lupu
avils N lupuke } "obit ætatis N."

zilachnke, "sepelitur."

zilachnke avils N, "sepelitur ætatis N."

zilachnuke lupuke, "sepelitur, obit."

avils machs N lupu, "obit ætatis mensis (menso) N."

avils thunesi N lupu, "obit ætatis dici (die) N."

.. *avenke lupum avils machs N*, "deponit cadaver aetatis mensis (mense) N."
eka suthi, "hic conditur."
eka suthi nesl, "hic conditur mortnus."
thui, "memoratur."
tular, "tumulus."

As a companion to the Etruscan epitaphs, whose examination I have now concluded, the longest of the very few Phrygian epitaphs that we possess is here subjoined, with its interpretation from the Armenian:*

Kelokes	*fenaflun*	*aftas*	*materes*	*sosesait*,
Celoces	sepulcrum	suæ	matris	facit,
materes	*Efeteksetis*	*Ofefinonoman.*		*Lachit*
matris	Ephetexetis	ex Ofefinone.		{ Sepelit { Vorat
ga	*materan*	*aresastin.*	*Bonok*	*akenanogafos*
terra	matrem	præstantem.	Bonocus	illustris
erekun	*telatos*	*sostut;*	*Inanon*	*akenanogafos*,
usum	{ sepulcri { loci	vetat;	Inanon	illustris,
acr	*atanisen,*	*kursaneson*		*tanegertos.*
vir	judicialis,	destructionem		ædificii.

Cicero writes (*De Leg.*, ii, 26): "De sepulcris nihil est apud Solonem amplius, quam 'ne quis ea deleat, neve alienum inferat'; poenaque est, 'si quis bustum

---

* It was said by Eudorus (ap. Eustathium): Ἀρμένιοι τὸ γένος ἐν Φρυγίας, καὶ τῇ φωνῇ πολλὰ φρυγίζουσιν. As might be expected from a contemporary of Xenophon and Agesilaus, and one who was himself a traveller, Eudorus is right about language: but the Phrygians probably came from Armenia, not the Armenians from Phrygia.

(nam id pnto appellari τύμβον), aut monumentum, aut columnam violarit, dejecerit, fregerit.'" This passage, as well as ancient epitaphs in general, will shew that the Armenian brings out a good sense for the whole of the Phrygian epitaph; in which Bonok may have been the lord of the ground, and Inanon a judge of the district. Both Bonok and Inanon were *illustres*, or "noblemen," while Ccloces was an untitled man, perhaps a dependent or client of Bonok.

Fenaft-un, "sepulcrum," with an objective termination, is the Armenian *anavth*, or *anóth*, "vessel, pot, box, *arca*, ἀγγείον," and probably the Albanian *ouńth*, "a pot."

Aft-as, "suæ," implies *af*, "he," which corresponds to the Kurdish *au*, "this, that," and to the Armenian *iv*, "he," which is found in *ivr*, "of him," and also "his." The genitive of *ivr*, "his," is *ivroy*.

The root of *sosesait*, "facit," may be discerned, most likely, in the Armenian *sós*-aphel, "to handle, manier"; the composition of sosesait (and possibly its root) in the Armenian sar-*as*-el, "to form, to shape" (root *sar*, in Persian *sdź*); and the conjugation of sosesa*it* in the Armenian t-*ay*, "he gives, dat." The Phrygian, like the Latin, retains the final *t*, which is dropped in Greek, Armenian, and Etruscan, as also in Italian and Spanish.

Ofefinonoman, "ex Ofefinone," has a termination which finds a parallel in the Armenian *dmané*, "from this," and yayg*man*, "in the morning (*ayg*)."

Lachit is a verb of the *i* conjugation, which, if rendered "verat," is explained from the Armenian *laké*, "he swallows"; and, if rendered "sepelit," contains the root of the Etruscan zi*lach*nke, which is found in the Armenian *etng*, "fossa" (*ante*, p. 84).

Gu, "tellus," is the Aryan word which appears in Greek as γῆ, in Gaelic as *ce*, in German as *gau*, in Sanskrit as *go*, and in Armenian as *kav*, "clay," and *gav(ar)*, "province."

Ares-astin, "præstantem," contains the Armenian *yarağ*, "before," *arağ*, "front," *arağ-in*, "first," combined with a termination like that of the Armenian *nav-ast*, or *nav-asti*, "a sailor." Indeed, *arcs-ast-in* might be obtained from the Armenian *yarağ-anal*, "præire, to excel," just as *ovr-ast*, "a denier," is obtained from *ovr-anal*, "to deny."

Frek-un, "usum," would contain the Greek ἐργ-, and the Armenian *erk*, "toil," *herk*, "cultivation."

Aken-anogafos, "illustris," is derived from the same word as the Armenian *akan-avor*, "illustrious," namely, *akn*, "an eye"; and may perhaps contain also the Armenian *angov*, "worthy of," so as to signify "worthy of respect, honourable."

Telatos, if interpreted "sepulcri," may be allied to the Armenian *that-el*, "to bury," and *thatar*, "an earthen vessel"; and to the Etruscan *tular*, "a tomb": or, if interpreted "loci," to the Armenian *teti*, "place," which seems akin to the root of *thatar*, namely, *that*, "tellus." The form of *telatos* is just like that of τέρατος.

Sostut, "vetat," is a verb of the *u* conjugation, and = Armenian *sasté*, "he reprehends."

Aer (the word is doubtful) seems the Armenian *ayr*, "man."

Atan-isen, "judicialis," contains the Armenian *atean*, "tribunal, court of justice," and is equivalent in meaning to the Armenian *aten-akan*, "judicial, magistrate, judge," or to the Armenian *aten-akal*, "magistrate, senator."

Kursan-eson, "destructionem," is explained from the Armenian *korzan-el*, "to destroy," and *korzun-outhivn*, "destruction." The termination *-es-* rather resembles the Armenian *-ič* "-tor," as in *tov-ič*, "giver, da-tor." If *kursaneson* signifies "destroyer" or "injurer," *erekun* ought to signify "nser," not "use."

Tanegert-os, "ædificii," is a compound like *Tigrano-certa*, and is composed of the Armenian words, *tovn*, gen. *tan*, "a house," and *kert*, "building."

That *akenanogafos* is a title may be seen also from the epitaph on the tomb of King Midas:—

Ates arkiaefas akenanogafos Midai gafagtaei fanaktei edaes.

Here *arkiaefas* might signify "royal," from the Armenian *archay*, "king"; or could perhaps be better explained from the Armenian *yarg*, "value, esteem, dignity," *yargi*, "respectable," *yargoy*, "honourable, precious, reverend." *Gafagtaei* may be derived from the Armenian *gah*, "throne," and possibly be equivalent to the Armenian *gahakži*, the dative of *gahakž*, "sharer of a throne, fellow-sovereign"; or else contain the Armenian *gta-nel*, "to acquire, to have." For *fanoktei*, "king," see *infra*, p. 79. *Edaes*, "posnit," is a first aorist, like ἔθηκε or ἔζησε, while the Armenian *ed*, "posuit," is a second aorist, like ἔθη. The terminations of the Armenian first aorist active, in the third person singular, are *-eaṡ* and *-aṡ*, according to the conjugation. It usually wants the augment; but in *e-k-eaṡ*, "he lived," and *e-b-aṡ*, "he opened," we meet with forms completely like the Phrygian *e-d-aes*, "posnit." *Edaes* terminates two other short inscriptions, so that its meaning is clear.

I have already noticed the identity of the Phrygian ἔλυμος, "αὐλός," with the Armenian *stégn*, "reed." Another Phrygian plant-name was *remenia*, "hyoscyamus, henbane," which is merely mentioned in my Armenian dictionary as "a poisonous plant." But *-eni* forms names of trees in Armenian, as in *keṛaseni*, "a cherry-tree"; and the same language has *ṛem-akal* = *okh-akal*, "malignant," and therefore implicitly *ṛem* = *okh*, "malice." Yet the nearest word to *remenia* is the Sanskrit *ramaṇíya*, "pleasant, a charm," of which the root is *rám*, "love, delight." Henbane may have been used in philtres. An almost synonymous Sanskrit word, *priya*, "gratus," might explain the first element of the Dacian πρια-δῆλα, "ἄμπελος μέλαινα," of which the second element, δῆλα, is the Armenian *det*, "herb, medicine." The Phrygian σοῦσα, "λείρια," is obviously Semitic, but may have been derived immediately from the Armenian *sousan*, "lily." Ζέλκια, the Phrygian for λάχανα, resembles more than one Armenian word: as *ẓatik* (in composition *ẓatk-*), "flower"; *ẓatk*, "stalk"; *setkh*, "melon," = Albanian *śalkyi*. The relics of the

Lydian language supply us with two names of the same kind. One is ἄκυλον, "βάλανον πρινίνην," which may be compared with the German *eichel*, and tho Armenian *katin*, "acorn." Tho other is μυσός, "ὀξύη, beech"; a word which seems allied to the Abkhasian *mića*, "wood"; to the Sanskrit *mićata*, "sandal-wood"; and to the Armenian *mośay*, "tamarisk." The name of *Mysia* was supposed to be derived from μυσός. If we may trust Homer, the tamarisk was common in tho Troad (*Il.*, vi. 39; x. 466; xxi. 18, 350). Herodotus mentions it in Lydia (vii. 31), where Mr. Hamilton (vol. ii, p. 144) speaks of "thickets of tamarisk." There was a *Mæsia Silva* in Etruria, not far from Rome. The Proper Thracian supplies us with three plant-names. Βρίζα was the name of a plant like τίφη, of which the thema is τῖφος, "marsh, stagnant water." The Sanskrit *vrîhi*, and the Armenian *brinj*, "rice," and the Rhæto-Romance *rüscha*, "grass growing in water," would be akin to βρίζα. Tho second Thracian plant-name is κῆμος, "ὄσπριόν τι." Tho Sanskrit has *kâmin*, "a climbing plant," and the Tuschi has *kam*, = Georgian *kuma*, "dill." The Bessi supply the third Thracian plant-name, ἀσâ, "βήχιον, tussilago, colts-foot," which is plainly allied to the Armenian *haz*, Sanskrit *kâsu*, "βήξ, tussis"; and, as the Germans call "coltsfoot" huf-*lattich*, the Armenian *hazar*, "lettuce," might also be compared with *haz* and ἀσâ. Tho change of the Sanskrit *kâsa* into tho Armenian *haz* is like the change, in Florentine pronunciation, of *casa* into χasa or *hasa*. Professor Max Müller has noticed the apparent affinity of the Dacian μαντεῖα, "*sentis, rubus,* bramble, blackberry," to the Albanian; in which language we find *man, mandē,* "a mulberry, a mulberry-tree," *mandü pherrë (pherrē,* "bramble"), "a blackberry." In Armenian we have, according to Rivola, *mandak,* "genus herbæ"; and there is likewise the Armenian *man-anekh,* "mustard," and the Ossetic *män-ārth,* "a raspberry, *rubus idæus.*" Perhaps the original meaning of *man-, mand-,* or μαντ-, is "berry"; and the root may appear in the Sanskrit *maṇḍala,* "orbis, circuitus," and in the Armenian *man,* "a round," which is also found in the expression *man pltoṣ,* "blossom of fruits *(pltoṣ)*." All these words might have belonged to a race who spoke dialects closely allied to the Sanskrit, as the Armenian is, and who proceeded from a country in the position of Armenia. The Dacian plant-names (*ante,* pp. 8, 9) have exhibited still more striking Armenian affinities.

CHAPTER III.

ETRUSCAN VOTIVE INSCRIPTIONS.

THE principle on which the argument in the preceding chapter has been conducted is, to determine in general the sense of each word without regard to its sound or form, and then to see what language or languages can explain that sense. This was possible in epitaphs, but is not so in votive forms of expression, or at least not so readily and completely. The shortest and, I think, the best mode of proceeding here will be, to exhibit at once the interpretations at which I have arrived, and then to prove their correctness, or at least their fitness.* I shall begin therefore by laying before the reader the three longest Etruscan votive inscriptions, accompanied by the interpretations which I put upon them. The first is on a statue, now at Leyden (Micali, *Mon.*, tav. XLIII; Lanzi, vol. ii, p. 455). It runs thus:—

Velias	Fanaknal	thuf-lthas	alpan	lenache
Veliæ	Fanacia-natæ	signum-precis	supplex	facessit
klen	kecha	tuthines	llen-acheis.	
pia	expiat	gratiæ	debitum-pretium.	

All the terms used here will be subsequently ex-

---

* The other or analytical process was adopted in my *Armenian Origin of the Etruscans* (1861).

plained. The proper name, *Fanak*, deserves observation, on account of its resemblance to the Phrygian *fanaktei* (*ante*, p. 74), = Greek ἄνακ-τι, and of the connexion of those words with the Armenian *nakh*, "first," and with the *naqa*, "king," of the Persian inscriptions. In the Milesian traditions reported by Pausanias, *Anax*, = Armenian *nakh*, "first," is the Autochthon and the son of Earth (*Ge*). Ἄναξ would be a Thracian, not a Hellenic word: at least it is Armenian, and is not Latin. The father of St. Gregory, the Apostle of Armenia, was said to be a Parthian called *Anak*.

The next long inscription, on the base of the statue of "the Orator" in the Uffizi at Florence (Micali, *Mon.*, tav. XLIV; Lanzi, vol. ii, p. 468), is as follows:—

Aulesi	Metelis	Ve.	Vesial	klensi ken
Aulus	Metellus	Veli filius	Vesia-natus	pius nt
fleres	teke	sansl	tenine	tuthines chiseliks.*
donum	ponit	libens	fert	gratiæ monumentum.

The proper name, *Vesia*, may be compared with the Armenian *wés*, "superbus." *Ken*, "nt," seems found in the Armenian *kén*, which is, however, only employed in composition. There are in Armenian two triads of terms signifying "as, like":—

or-bar, or-pés, or-kén——hi-bar, hi-pés, hi-kén.

Or signifies "who, which," and so would *hi*, which the Armenian *him*, "quare," = Sanskrit *kim*, "quare," shews to be identical with the Sanskrit *ki*, "who,

---

* In the original, *chiseliks*. I have changed the *v* (F) into *s* (E), as in the case of *tierr*, "thirty."

which," = Albanian *kyë*. *Bar* means "modus" in Armenian, and *-pēs* = Sanskrit *peça*, "forma." All the six terms above therefore signify "quomodo"; and *kēn* may thus be interpreted "ut."

The following is the third long votive inscription, and accompanies a statue of Apollo (Lanzi, vol. ii, p. 446:—

mi   fleres   Epul   (a)fe   Aritimi
mo   donum   Apollini   ot   Artemidi
Fasti   R(u)fr(u)a   turke   klen   kecha.
Fausta   Rufria   dat   pia   expiat.

Afe, "and," would be identical with the Armenian *ev*, "and," which Bötticher refers to the Sanskrit *abhi*, "ad, versus," = Greek ἐπί. But the word is doubtful, and is not found elsewhere. Fabretti reads *svulare* instead of *Epul afe*.

On a candelabrum (Lanzi, vol. ii. p. 421) there is also this expression:—

Au.   Velskus   thup-lthas   alpan   turke.*
Aulus   Veliscus   signum-precis   supplex dat.

I will next give a complete list of Etruscan votive forms, omitting proper names, and reversing in three instances, for the sake of comparison, the order in which two words occur. The list would be this:—

---

* *Alpan turke* terminates two other votive forms. Fabretti, 1051, 1052. In the Etruscan kecha, "expiat," turke, "dat," suthi, "condi tur," and lupu, "obit," we have examples of the four Armenian conjugations in a, e, i, and u (ou); as in the Armenian tay, "gives," ate, "hates," lini, "is," and lizov, "licks." Three of the four appear in the Phrygian sosesait, lachit, and sostut (*ante*, pp. 72, 73).

1. *kana*
2. *suthina*
3. *flezrl*
4. *fleres* ....*tlen-asies*
5. *fleres-zck* .... *sansl*
6.   *turuke*
7. *fleres*   *turke*
8. *fleres*   *turke*   *klen*   *kecha*
9. *alpan thup-lthas turke*   [*acheis*
10. *alpan thuf-lthas lenache klen kecha tuthines tlen-*
11. *klensi fleres*   *teke*   *sansl tenine tuthines chise-*
                                                                [*liks*

The next step in the argument will be to give the meaning of these words, as deduced mainly from the Armenian; and to show, as in the case of sepulchral expressions, that such meanings make Etruscan votive forms correspond in sense to the forms used by the ancients. I therefore subjoin this comparative list of ancient votive terms:—

LATIN & GREEK.   ETRUSCAN.

Εἰκών   *kana*, " simulacrum, statua."
Ἄγαλμα   *zek*, " statua, figura."
Ἀνάθημα   *suthina*, " sacrificium."
Εὐχῆς ἕνεκα   *thup-lthas*, " signum-precis."
Ex voto   *fleres*, " donum."
Donum   *flezrl*, " datum."
Votum
Libens   *sansl*, " libens."
            klen, klensi, " pius."
            alpan, " supplex, ἱκέτης."

LATIN & GREEK.	ETRUSCAN.
ἀνέθηκε	*tenine,* " fert."
Posuit	*teke,* " ponit," or " facit."
Retulit	
Fecit	*lenache,* " facessit, fieri facit."
Dedit	*turke,* " dat."
Solvit	*kecha,* " expiat," or " solvit."
Dedicavit	
Consecravit	
Χαριστήρια	*tuthines chiseliks,* "gratiæ monumentum."
Merito	*tuthines tlen-acheis,* "gratiæ debitum-[pretium."
	tlen-asies, ... dobitum-[pretium."

The meanings assigned to the Etruscan words are thus suitable, and therefore likely to be true; and this probability may be still further shown by the following inscription, which is found in Gruter, p. xlvii:—

To *precor** Alcido *sacris* invicte *peractis*
Rite† tuis *lætus dona ferens meritis*‡
Hæc tibi nostra potest tenuis perferre camina
Nam *grates dignas*§ tu potes efficere
Sumo *libens*‖ *simulacra*¶ tuis quæ *munera*** cilo
Aris Urbanus *dedicat*†† ipso sacris.

I shall now show how the meanings assigned to the

---
* *Alpan* † *Klen, klensi.*
‡ *Sansl tenine tuthines chiseliks, klen kecha tuthines tlen-acheis.*
§ *Tlen-asies.* ‖ *Sansl.* ¶ *Kana, tek.*
** *Heres, suthina* †† *Turke, kecha.*

Etruscan words are obtained, almost entirely from the Armenian:—

Kana (1) "simulacrum" (Lanzi, vol. ii, pp. 465, 466). Gaelic *caon*, "simulacrum;" or Armenian *k-al*, "sistere," *-an*, Armenian termination, = Sanskrit *-ana*. *Kana* is found on statues.

Suthina (2), "sacrificium."

Tuthines (10, 11), "gratiæ, donationis, χάριτος." These words are of the utmost significance. *Suthina* is found alone on a number of objects; among others, on a statue (Micali, *Mon.*, tav. xxxv, 9), and on the back of a patera (tav. xlviii): it is also sometimes accompanied by a proper name (Fabretti, p. clxxxiii). The most probable meaning of *suthina* is obviously "a votive offering;" and it would therefore be duly explained from the Sanskrit *hu*, "Diis offerre, sacrificare," just as the Etruscan *suth-i*, "is buried," was explained from the Sanskrit *hud*, "coacervare, submergi" (*ante*, p. 62). Though it would seem probable, at first sight, that *suthi* and *suthina* were cognate words, yet they need be no more so than *potis* and *potio*; *lot*, *lutus*, and *lotion*; *rat* and *ration*. We may also fairly conclude that *suthina* does not mean "tomb" or "urn;" for such an inscription as *Larth Seties suthina* is found on *several* vases, "in *nonnullis* vasis" (Fabretti, 2095 *quinq. B*). The ashes of a deceased person would not be distributed among a number of vases: nor, indeed, does there seem any sense but "votive offering" which will explain the fact of *suthina* being found as a single word on statues, pateræ, and, as in Fabretti, *quinq. A*, "in nonnullis monumentis aheneis," discovered at one place. As therefore *suthi* appears on tombs, it is probable that *suthi* and *suthina* have no etymological connexion; and it is also probable that, while *suthina* is a nominative, *tuthines* is the genitive of a similar nominative *tuthina*, where the termination is the same as that of *suthina*, but the root different, just as we find in Latin *natio* and *ratio, motio* and *notio*. We should thus have these words in Etruscan:—

su-thina, or else *s(u)-uthina*, " sacrificium."
tu-thina, or else *t(u)-uthina*, " . . . ."

In the termination -*uthina*, an Armenian would at once recognise his native termination -*outhivn*, which is so common as to occur three times in the Lord's Prayer, as well as in twelve nouns derived from *nav*, "a ship," and in fifteen derived from *mard*, "a man." The Sanskrit *hu*, "Diis offerre, sacrificare," becomes the Armenian *zoh*, which would be *suh* in Etruscan orthography; while the root of the Etruscan *t(u)-uthina* or *t-uthina* is found in the Armenian *tov* or *t-*, "give;" for "d-are" is *t-al*, and "d-atus" is *tov-eal*, in Armenian. We have, indeed, both the Etruscan words in Armenian: for "human *sacrifice*" is marda-*zohovthivn*, and "*giving* of homage" is barka-*tovovthivn*, in that language.

The final vowel in *suthin-a* would be dropped in Armenian, as may be seen by such an instance as *kin*, "γυνή," with which may be compared the Etruscan *kina*, that occurs in the beginning of an inscription at Volterra:—

Titesi Kalesi kina Ks Mestles.....

The Etruscan proper name, *Mestles*, resembles the name of the Mæonian leader, Μέσθλης (Il. II, 864), and that of the Iberian town, Μεστλῆτα, mentioned by Ptolemy. *Mes-* may be the Armenian *mez*, "great," = Zend *mazó*, = Sanskrit *mah(at)*, another example of the change of the Sanskrit *h* into a sibilant.

The following table will exhibit the affinity between the Armenian and Etruscan in several points already considered; and may likewise explain, to some extent, by showing in what manner the Armenian uses infinitives and participles as nouns, how the Etruscan comes to have so many *l* terminations:—

ARMENIAN ROOTS & WORDS.	ETRUSCAN ROOTS & WORDS.
souz, "cond-ere."	*suth,* = Sanskrit *hud.*
zoh, "sacrifice."	*su,* = Sanskrit *hu.*
tov, "give."	*tu.*
av, "age, increase."	*av,* = Sanskrit *av.*
rah, "go."	*ri,* = Sanskrit *ri.*
tes, "sight."	
tes-ové, gen. *tes-ći,* "inspector."	
tes-avor, "apparent."	
tes-il (videri), "appearance."	*av-il,* "age."
tes-avor-il, "to appear."	*r(i)-il,* "year."
tes-an-el, "to see."	
tes-an-el, "appearance."	
tes-ot (videns), "prophet."	
tes-an-ot (videns), "prophet."	
tes-outhivn, "sight."	*s(u)-uthina,* "sacrificium."
tes-ć-outhivn, "inspection."	*t(u)-uthines,* "donationis."

tes-an-el-ovthivn, "visibility."
tes-ot-ovthivn, "sight."
tes-an-ot-ovthivn, "sight."
tes-an-eli, "visurus, videndus."
tesanelich, "the eyes, sight."

These last two Armenian forms will illustrate in its place the Etruscan *chiseliks.*

Flezrl (3), "datum."
Fleres (4, 5, 7, 8, 11), "donum."

I have met with *flezrl* only once: it occurs on the back of a statue (Micali, *Mon.,* tav. xxxiii). The analogy of *fleres* would lead us to expect *flerzl* instead of *flezrl,* while we should infer from *nesl,* "mortuus," that *flezrl* or *flerzl* is probably a participle. On a patera in Lanzi (tav. xi), a pedestal with a bust is inscribed *flere.* The connexion with *fleo* and *ploro* is most likely a correct one. The Armenian gives:—*eter,* "fletus" —*aters,* "precis"—*overz,* "donum"—and *eterzeal, otorzeal,* and *overzeal,* "datus, oblatus." The initial vowels here may be due to the circumstance, that few Armenian words are allowed to begin with $t, = \chi\lambda, =$ Welsh *ll,* which the English pronunciation converts into *thl* or *fl.* The Armenian *etag* (*ante,* p. 84) is an instance of a vowel being prefixed to *t.* The *f* in *fleres* may represent the aspirate χ contained in *t.* But compare also the Armenian *lov,* "*flea, floh,*" where *f* before *l* is entirely dropped. In *li,* "πλέ-ος," *p* is dropped.

Tlen-asies (4)
Tlen-acheis (10) } "debitum pretium."

Gaelic *dligh,* "debe;" *dlighe,* "lex, debitum;" *dleas,*

"officium ;" root *dl-*, in Etruscan *tl-*: *-ean*, Armenian adjectival termination.

Armenian *aséch*, "pretium," a plural noun: in the objective, the final *-ch* becomes *-s*. Ossetic *achos* " a aum due ;" *achza*, "money." Greek ἀξία. Compare a*ch*eis and a*s*ies with the two Armenian forms for "daughter," do*kh*t and dov*s*tr.

Turuke (6)
Turks (7, 8, 9) } " dat. δωρεῖ."

Armenian *tovrch*, "gift," a plural noun, of which the root or base is *tovr*: it is found in *phaṛ-a-tré*, "he gives glory (*phaṛ*)." As already noticed, a great many Etruscan verbs seem to terminate in *-ke*, like *tur-ke*; a form apparently used by the Lydians, as the Lydian βάσκε, "ἐξεθόαζε," would = the Armenian *waz-ér*, "he was rushing." Another example of such a form is supplied by the picture which forms the frontispiece to the second volume of Mr. Dennis' *Etruria*. It represents the self-devotion of Alcestia to death for her husband, and is accompanied by this inscription ;—

eka erske nak achrum flerthrke.

Eka has already been interpreted "here" or "ecce," from the Armenian *ahá*, "lo !" The Georgian has *aha*, "ecce ;" *ach*, "hic ;" and *acha*, "ibi." *Ers-ke*, as we know the subject of the picture, may be considered as equivalent to the Armenian *eres-é*, "she offers herself." *Nak* may mean "to," like the German *nach*, the Hungarian *nak*, and the Tuschi *naqw*; and a similar word would appear in the Armenian *nakh*, "first, before," which is both adjective and adverb, and has in composition nearly the force of the German *nach*, as in the

Armenian *nakhanj*, "envy." And thus, as *fler-thrke* would be already explained under *fleres* (p. 86) and *turke* (p. 87), the whole inscription would probably mean: "Lo! she offers herself to Acheron as a devoted (or 'suppliant') gift." As a comparison of forms, notice that *thrke* elides the vowel in *turke*, as the Armenian *srbé*, "ho sanctifies," elides the vowel *ov*, = *u*, in *sovrb*, "holy," = Sanscrit *çubhra*, "splendidus, albus." Compare the Sabine *cyprum*, "bonum," and the Etruscan *Cypra*, "Juno," which would be a Sabine word.

Zek (5), "statua, figura."

Armenian *zev*, *zevak*, "form, figure." *Zek* might likewise bo rendered "brought," from the Armenian *zgel*, = German *ziehen*; or "produced," from the Armenian *zagel*, = German *zeugen*. Perhaps *zek*, which only occurs once, should be *zeke*, "brings," = Armenian *zgé*.

Sansl (5, 11), "libens."

Armenian *znzavt*, *znzót*, or *znzot*, "gaudens, libens." The inscription (5), when completed, is: *fleres zek(e) sansl kver*. It is found on the statue of a boy. I should interpret *kver*, "soror," guided by such Latin inscriptions as:—

D.M.C. Egnatio Epicteto et C. Egnatio Floro modesta *soror*.

Fortunato fratri pientissimo fecerunt *sorores*.

The Armenian for "sister" is *choyr*, which is pronounced like the English *queer*, and gives *cher* in the genitive. The Persian is *khwaher*; the Welsh, *chwaer*;

and the Breton, *choar*. On another statue of a boy, with the inscribed arm unfortunately nearly broken off (Micali, *Mon.*, tav. XLIV), is this fragment of an inscription:—

..... as velusa
..... is kelvansl
..... s *kver* thvethli
..... klan

As the Etruscan *Thanchvil* is the Latin *Tanaquil*, the Etruscan *kver* would probably be represented by *quer* in Latin. In the votive inscription, fleres tlen-asies sver, sver may = *k*ver, as tlen-asies seems = tlen-*ach*ois (*ante*, p. 86).

If the Etruscan *sansl* and *nesl* be "libens" and "necatus," and if *avil* and *ril* be infinitives as well as nouns, we should find these terminations in four languages:—

	ETRUSCAN.	ARMENIAN.	PERSIAN.	SANSKRIT.
Infinitive ...	-l	-l	-dan	-tum
Pres. Part....	-l	-t	-n	-(n)t
Past. Part....	-l	-l	-dah	-ta

The Lydian κανδαύλ(ης) would exhibit the present participle in a third Thracian dialect (*ante*, p. 7).

Klen (8, 10) ⎫ " pius, rito," i.o. " with due religious
Klensi (11) ⎭ rites."

For the termination of *klensi*, which distinguishes it from *klen*, compare the Armenian *layn* and *laynśi*, "broad;" or *bolor*, "a circle," and *bolorśi*, "round;" and for the meaning of *klen*, compare the Gaelic *glan* and the Welsh *glân*, *glain*, "pure, holy, clean, beautiful, fair;" and perhaps the Armenian *getani*, "fair, decent."

On a tomb at Vulci (Micali, *Mon. Ined.*, tav. LIX) the sculptured figure of a man stands in a rock-hewn blank doorway, and is surrounded by an inscription which may be interpreted as follows:—

Eka suthik   Velus Ezpus klensi kerinu
"Hic tumulum Velus Ezpus pius sculpit."

For *suthik* may bo considered as a diminutive of *suthi*, "a tomb" *(ante*, p. 69), like the Armenian *masnik*, "a particle," from *masn*, "a part;" or *lovsik*, "a little light," from *loys*, "light." *Ker-in-u*, like *lup-u (ante*, p. 33), would be an Armenian verb of tho *ov* or *u* conjugation, derived from a root *ker*, which may be allied to *cher-el*, "to scrape," or *gër-el*, "to write," or *kōṛ-el*, "to hammer, to carve." For the *-in-* in *kerinu*, compare Armenian forms like *lizané*, *lizé*, *lizov*, *lezov*, "he licks"—*gotanay*, *goté*, "he steals"— *kheṛanay*, *kheṛi*, "he insults"—*kamenay*, *kami*, "he wishes." Similar *n* forms are common in Aryan languages. *Lini*, "he is," supplies another instance in Armenian.

Kecha (8, 10), "expiat, consecrat," or olso "solvit." Armenian *chahé*, "expiat"———*chaké*, "solvit." There is also *kahé*, "parat." See *ante*, p. 37, No. 2340: *klalum ke* ..., "funera ....."

Tenine (11), "fert, offert."

Armenian *tani*, "fert, reddit, tenet." *Ten-in-e* would bo a form like *ker-in-u*, just noticed, but in an *e*, not a *u* conjugation. The simpler form is *tenu (ante*, p. 36, note †). Compare the Armenian *písnov*, = *písné*, = *písé*, "he considers."

Alpan (9, 10), "supplex, ἱκέτης, flehend."

Armenian *otb*, "fletus:" -*an*, -*ean*, Armenian adjectival terminations. The letters *o* and *b* are wanting in Etruscan.

Teke (11), "facit," or else "ponit."

Lapponic *takk-et*, Fin *tek-ä*, "facere." Sanskrit *takś*, "facere, fabricare, findere;" *takśan*, "faber lignarius." Armenian *thak*, "a hammer, a mallet;" *thak-el*, "to beat, to ram." Latin *tignum*, *tigillum*. Greek τέκτων, τέχνη.

Te-ke might also be regarded as an Etruscan verb in -*ke* from a root *t*- "placing." This Aryan root is in Armenian *d-*, and *dë-né* is "ponit," an *n* form like the Etruscan *ten-inu* and *ker-inu*.

Thup-llhas (9)
Thuf-llhas (10) } "signum precis, an *ex voto*."

Τύπος λιτής. Armenian *tophel*, *thopel*, *dophel*, "τύπτειν"——*atóthel*, "precari;" *itź*, "desiderium;" *ëtźal*, "desiderare." Though the Armenian avoids *t* as an initial, yet we find *tźali*, as well as *ëtźali*, "desiderandus." Τύπος illustrates *teke* by exhibiting the connexion between "striking," and "forming" or "making." As τύπος and λιτή are not Latin (for *typus* is borrowed), they would be Thracian rather than Hellenic words, if the Hellenes were an offshoot of the same Italian race to which the Umbrians and Oscans belonged.

Lenachs (10), "facessit."

Armenian *etanaké*, "modulatur;" *etanak*, "modus, forma;" *etanil* "fieri;" *linel*, "esse, fieri, existere." There is, besides, the suffix *-etén*, "fac(tus)," as in *osketén*, "made of gold *(oski)*".* In Armenian, the termination *-ak* is frequently causative, like the Sanskrit *-aka*: e.g. *é*, "existence;" *éak*, "creator;" so that, as *lin-el* is "fieri," *lin-aké* would be "fieri facit." If *lenache* be "facessit," *teke* would be "ponit" rather than "facit."

Chiseliks (11), "monumentum, in memoriam."

Armenian *yiselich*, "a memorial," the plural form of *yiseli*, of which the diminutive would be *yiselik* (a form like the Etruscan *suthik*), and its plural form *yiselikch*, in the objective *yiseliks*. *Yiseli* is the future participle of *yisel*, "to remember," of which the root is *yis*. Similar forms to *yiselich* are:—*talich*, "gift," *lselich*, "ear, audience," *empelich*, "beverage," and *tesanelich*, "sight, eyes" (*ante*, p. 86). But the existing Armenian forms derived from the root *khat*, "playing," will most clearly exemplify the supposed formation of *chiseliks* from a root *chis*.

ARMENIAN.	ETRUSCAN.
khat, "ludus."	*chis*
khatal, "ludere."	
khatali, "ludendus."	
khatalich, "ludus," i.e. "ludenda."	
khatalik, "ludus" (dimin.)	
khataliks, "ludos."	*chiseliks*

For the affinity between the Etruscan *chis* and the Armenian *yis*, compare the Armenian *khorzel*, *yorzel*,

---

* Cf. Lithuanian *auksas*, Prussian *ausis*.

"to seek." The Armonian *y* is aspirated.* In the mountains of Noricum there was a place called *Candalicæ*, which resembles the Armenian *khaṭ-alık* in form, and which may, by the aid of the root *cand*, "throttle" (*ante*, p. 7), be interpreted "gorgos," or "étranglements." The Albanian has *erëēli*, "honourable" (th. *ers*, "honour"), to compare with the Armenian *yargeli*, "venerandus." On the Noric *Elegium*, see *ante*, p. 66.

I have now completely gone through the votive words comprised in the forms at the beginning of the chapter (*ante*, p. 81). A few other words may be added to them. The first is the well-known *Tins-kvil*, which stands alone on three votive offerings (one of them the celebrated Chimæra), and in which the name of *Tina*, the Etruscan Jupiter, has long been recognised. *Tina* would be the Sanskrit *dina*, "day," a contraction of *divana* (Lassen) = *divan*, "day." The root is *div*, "to shine," which appears in the Armenian *tiv*, "day," in the Latin *dies*, *divum*, *divinus*, and, as already noticed, in the Albanian *diel* or *dil*, "the sun." It may be remarked here in passing, how the Albanian *vëlazër*, "brother," (which the plural shows to be the complete form of *vëla*, "brother"), enables us to pass from the Sanskrit *bhrâtṛi* to the Armenian *etbayr*, for *btayr*.

The Etruscan *kvil* in *Tins-kvil* seems = Armenian *khilay*, "gift;" which would make *Tinskvil* signify "Jovis donum, Jupiter's gift, a gift to Jupiter."

This word is found, together with some others, on

---
* We have also the Etruscan *kiem*, *chiem*, "five," to put by the side of the Armenian *hing*, "five," and *yi-sovn*, "fif-ty."

the beautiful candelabrum of Cortona. The inscription, which has slightly suffered from a fracture, appears to have run thus :—

thapna lusni (T)inskvil Athli(i) sulthn,

As *Ath* and *Athl* are both proper names in Etruscan (Lanzi, tom. II, p. 363 :—there is an Armenian district called *Athli*), the meaning of the inscription may be—
"A burner of light, offered to Tina, the work of Atilius."

Thapna, "καύστης,"—*lusni*, "luminis,"—and *salthn*, "cast, fonte, formatio, opus," may be thus explained:

1. Sanskrit *tap*, "burn," = Armenian *tap*, *thaph*: Sanskrit svap*na*, "sleep;" Armenian mas*n*, "part," ot*n*, "foot."

2. Armenian *loys*, "light;" *lovsin*, gen. *lovsni*, "the moon;"* *lovsn-thag* ("light-crown"), "the planet Jupiter."

3. *Salthn* might be explained either from the Armenian *sat-mn*, "an embryo," or from the Armenian *sat-el*, "to mix, to knead." The termination -*thn* may be a contraction of -*outhiun* (ante, p. 84). In *form*, *salthn* resembles the Armenian *sovrthn*, "orifico."†

---

* On a patera or mirror in Lanzi (tav. XII, No. 6) Diana is called *Losna*, a name remarkable for containing the non-Etruscan vowel o.

† The Etruscan *kech-* (ante, p. 90) and the Armenian *chah-* (or *chav-*; cf. Sanskrit *khav*, "purificari") would explain two words in Hesychius, of which the last might exhibit the *l* termination of the Armenian, Lydian, and Etruscan present participle (ante, p. 89) :—

Κυί(ης) or κόί(ης), "ἱερεὺς Καβείρων ὁ καθαίρων φονέα."
Κοιδλ(ης), "ἱερεύς."

CHAPTER IV.

THE INSCRIPTION OF CERVETRI.

In the two previous chapters, which have been devoted to the consideration of sepulchral and votive forms in Etruscan, the force of the argument is in a great measure derived from the fact, that the Armenian language enables us to explain the Etruscan words in such a manner as to make the sense of the Etruscan forms correspond closely to that of other ancient forms of the same kinds. The meaning assigned to the Etruscan words may sometimes be described as certain, as in the cases of *avil*, *ril*, and *leine*, and may be generally affirmed as more or less probable in every case; so that the argument in favour of the Armenian or Thracian affinities of the Etruscan becomes very strong. In the subject of the present chapter, there are no such analogies to guide us: there is no sense which we are bound to elicit from the Etruscan by the aid of the Armenian, if the intimate relationship between the two languages is to be maintained. That the inscription of Cervetri is Armenian, depends chiefly upon the singular closeness with which the Armenian fits it, and which is such that even the metre of the inscription, for it is written in verso, scarcely suffers at all, while a good and appropriate sense is brought out for it at the same time.

The Inscription of Cervetri, the ancient *Agylla* or *Cære*, is written on a pot or cup of antique black ware, capable of holding nearly a pint; and it consists of two hexameter verses, but with the words all run together. They should probably be divided thus:—

*mi ni kethu ma mi mathu mar am lisiai thipurenai
ethe erai sie epana mi nethu nastav helephu.*

As it might be objected that the lines are divided into words so as to adapt them to the Armenian, it may be as well to mention that my division of them is the same as that of Lepsius, with the exception that he reads *maram* instead of *mar am* in the first line, and *minethu* instead of *mi nethu* in the second, where I follow Dr. Donaldson. *Maram* may perhaps be preferable to *mar am*, as will ultimately appear: but, if we read *mi ni kethu* and *mi mathu* with Lepsius, then *mi nethu* seems more probable than *minethu*. As we have already met with *mi*, "I," in Etruscan, it may reasonably be conjectured that the cup is made to speak of itself, and that it affirms of *muthu* what it denies of *kethu*. Again, as the Etruscan is an Aryan language, it will be at once suspected that *mathu* means "wine," for such a word occurs in a great number of Aryan dialects, from the English *mead* to the Sanskrit *madhu*.

With this slight clue to the tenor of the inscription, I will now proceed to interpret it word for word, as I have divided it:—

1. *Mi,* " I."

The Armenian for "I" is *es;* for "me," (z)*is* : but *me*, "I," and *me*, "me," exist implicitly in the Armenian plurals, *mech,* "wo" (= Lithuanian *més*), and (z)*mez,* "ns." For *dov,* "thou," makes *dovch,* "ye"; and the Armenian nominative plural is formed by the addition of *-ch* to the singular, and the accusative plural by that of *-s*.

Welsh and Gaelic *mi,* "I"; Georgian *me,* "I": etc.

2. *Ni,* "not."

Armenian *mi* = Greek $\mu\eta$ = Latin *ne*.

Welsh and Gaelic *ni,* "not." Behistun Persian *niya,* "not." Persian *mah, nah,* "not."

3. *Kethu,* "of water"; less probably, "of milk."

The Armenian *get,* "river," *kath,* "drop," *kith,* "milking," and *kathn,* "milk," are thus declined :—

Nominative ...... *get**	*kath*	*kith*	*kathn.*
Genitive .... *getoy*	*kathi*	*kthoy*	*kathin.*
Dative .... *getoy*	*kathi*	*kthoy*	*kathin.*
Ablative .... *getoy*	*kathē*	*kthoy*	*kathinē.*
Instrumental ...*getow*	*kathiv*	*kthow*	*kathamb.*

There is in Etruscan prose a remarkable deficiency of vowels, which does not appear in the Inscription of Cervetri; a difference which has led to the inference that the language of the Inscription of Cervetri is not Etruscan.† But this inference is too hasty, for the

---

* Armenian infinitives are declined completely, like *get*.

† "This (the Inscription of Cervetri) is neither Latin, nor Greek, nor Umbrian, nor Oscan. It is equally certain that it is not Etruscan ; since in that tongue harsh unions of consonants

same peculiarity exists in Armenian, where the vowel ŏ, which has the same sound as the Sanskrit *a*, is continually understood in prose, where it would be expressed in poetry. Auchor says of this Armenian letter: "Entre deux ou plusieurs consonnes elle est toujours sousentenduo; mais dans la division des mots *elle se met actuellement, comme aussi dans la poésie*." Sir Henry Rawlinson, in his explanation of the Persian Cuneiform Inscriptions (p. 55), writes: "The short sound of *a* was *optionally* inherent in all the consonants of the (ancient) Persian alphabet. This principle of organisation is common to every single branch of Arian Palæography, with the exception of the Zend." The Armenians and Etruscans exercised such an option by dropping in prose the short *a*, = Armenian *ĕ*, while the Phrygians preferred expressing it. In Sanskrit, the short *a* is *necessarily* implied in every consonant or combination of consonants, when unaccompanied by the mark *Virâma*, or the sign of some other vowel.

An Etruscan word where the deficiency of vowels is particularly great is *trutnvt*, which seems in a bilingual inscription (Lanzi, vol. ii. p. 565) to correspond to *haruspex*, and may be composed of the root or base

---

abound, while in this the distribution of vowels is as well proportioned as in the Negro-languages: moreover none of the well-known Etruscan words here occur."—Newman's *Regal Rome*, p. 7. *Mi*, "I, me," does occur in the Inscription of Cervetri: nor is there any reason why two verses on a drinking-cup should contain any votive or sepulchral words.

of *trutinor*, with the Armenian termination -*ovaṛ*,
= Sanskrit and Zend -*vat*. But though in *trutnvt* there
is only one vowel to six consonants, yet the same proportion is observed in two Armenian words of similar
sound: in *trtnǧel*, "to murmur," and in *θrθnǧuk*,
"sorrol," gen. *θrθnǧki*.* In two of the Armenian
words cited above to explain the Etruscan *kethu*, namely
kthoy and *kthow*, there is an *ö* deficient, and they
would be written in poetry *kēthoy* and *kēthow*; or in
Etruscan orthography, as the Etruscans had no *o*,
kethu in both cases. *Getoy* and *getow* would become
in like manner *ketu*, as the Etruscans had no medial
consonants.

Gaelic *cith, gith*, "imber"; *cè*, gen. *cèithe*, "flos
lactis." Albanian *cheth*, "stillaro, fundero." Latin
gutta.

4. *Ma*, "but."

Armenian *na*, "but, however, rather, in fact, rerum."
Sanskrit *aṁ*, "næ." Tuschi *ma*, "but." Lapponic
ma, "quidem."

5. *Mi*, "I."

6. *Mathu*, "of wine."

Armenian *math*, "syrup of grapes, raisiné, defrutum,"
which is declined like *get* (3). *Mathoy* would become
mathu in Etruscan.

German *meth*: English *mead*: Welsh *medd*: Greek

---

* I take this word to be the τιπρανδγερα of Dioscorides, one of
the five names by which the Romans knew *artemisia* or *mugwort*.
Like Pliny's *elegia* (*ante*, p. 66), it might possibly have been borrowed from Etruria.

μέθυ: Zend *mathu*, "wine": Sanskrit *madhu*, "honey, wine, intoxicating drink"; *mad*, "to be intoxicated"; *mada*, "intoxication, madness": Persian *may*, *mul*, "wine": Lydian μῶλαξ, "εἶδος οἴνου." Armenian *moli*, "mad, intoxicated"; *metr*, "honey," gen. *metov*: Greek μῶλυ.

7. *Mar*, "a pot" or "measure" (German *mass*).

Armenian *mar*, "a measure of liquids"—"μετρητής, firkin" (John ii. 6): Persian *mar*, "measure, number": Greek μάρις, "a measure containing six κοτύλαι (about three pints)":* Albanian *merö*, "overy liquid and dry measure": Lithuanian *mēra*, "measure": Russian *mjera*, "measure." Albanian *marr*, "to hold, to contain": Georgian *marani*, "a wine-cellar," = Armenian *maṛan*, Sanskrit, *má, mas*, "to measure." The Etruscan *mar* and *mathu* seem to contain Aryan roots of universal prevalence.

8. *Am*, "am."

Armenian ...*em*
Persian ......*am*
Behistun ......*amiya*
Zend ....*ahmi*   } "I am."
Albanian ......*yam*
Greek ....εἰμί
Sanskrit ......*asmi*

9. *Lisiai*, "for the tongue."

Armenian ...*lezov*
Lithuanian ...*lėžuwis*   } "a tongue."
Hebrew ......*lašon*

---

* Μάρις may be a Thracian word; and the Latin *dolium* appears in like manner = Armenian *doyl*, "bucket."

Armenian ...$\begin{cases} lezoul \\ lizoul \\ lizel \\ lizanel \end{cases}$ "to lick."

Lithuanian ......*lëżu*
Persian ....*lisidan*

Persian ....*lis*
Sanskrit ....*lih* $\Big\}$ "*lick*" (root).

Observe the letter-change in the Sanskrit *lih* and the Etruscan *lis*-iai. The genitive and dative of the Armenian *lezov* (i. o. *lezu*) are *lezovi*. But the Etruscan *lisia*, "a tongue," would be declined more nearly like such borrowed Armenian proper names as *Angtia*, "England," gen. and dat. *Angtiay;* or *Anania*, "Ananias," gen. and dat. *Ananiay*.

10. *Thipurenai*, "for the thirsty" (tongue).

In *thip* we meet with a very common Aryan root for "heat." In Armenian this root is *tap* or *thaph*, which has been discerned before in the Etruscan *thapna* (*ante*, p. 94). The Armenian *tapean*, "burning, heated," would give the meaning of *thipurenai*, but the termination must be explained from such Armenian words as those which follow:—

$\begin{cases} hayr, \text{ "father."} \\ hayr\text{-}\'or\'en, \text{ " paternally."} \end{cases}$

$\begin{cases} archay, \text{ "king."} \\ archay\text{-}\'or\'en, \text{ " royally."} \end{cases}$

$\begin{cases} ham\text{-}ak, \text{ "entire, entirely ": root } ham, = \dot{o}\mu\langle\'o\varsigma\rangle. \\ ham\text{-}\'or\'en, \text{ " entire, entirely."} \\ ham\text{-}\'orini, \text{ gen. and dat. of } ham\text{-}\'or\'en. \end{cases}$

$\begin{cases} get, \text{ " beauty."} \\ get\text{-}a\text{-}y\'or\'en, \text{ " fair."} \end{cases}$

{ *órén,* " a law, a rule."
{ *órin-ak,* " example, type, form."
{ *yórin-el,* " to form, to shape."
{ *órin-akel,* " to form, to represent."*

Nearly similar terminations may be found in the Armenian words:—*Hay-erén,* " Armenian, Haïcan"— *phokh-arén,* "payment"—*kerp, kerp-aran,* "form, figure." There is no indication of genders in the Armenian language; but such proper names as *Athenas,* " Pallas," gen. and dat. *Athenay,* are declined like *thipurenai,* which would be a feminine adjective agreeing with *lisiai.*

11. *Ethe,* " if," or " when."†

Armenian ...*ethé*
Zend ....*yézi, yéidhi*
Behistun ......*yadiya*
Sanskrit ......*yadi* } " if."

---

* Compare with *órin-aké,* " he forms," the Etruscan verbs, *lenache, tur-ke* and *tur-uke, ers-ke, te-ke, silachn-ke* and *silachn-uke.* Such Armenian words as *hayr,* "father," and *mayr,* " mother," intimate that the Armenian language, in its earliest existent state, is not very ancient. Indeed, the oldest Armenian writings only date from about 400 A.D. For the Armenian forms for " daughter," " brother," and " sister," see *ante,* pp. 63, 88, 93. The Phrygian inscriptions, as might be expected, bear evidence of much higher antiquity; for in them we find *materes* and *materan,* = μητέρες and μητέρα, = *matris* and *matrem,* = Sanskrit *mâtaras* and *mâtaram.* Compare *materan* and *mayr* with *matrem* and *mère.* The Armenians have a word *orstr,* " son," which possesses the Aryan termination of pa-*ter,* ma-*ter,* and daugh-*ter,* and seems peculiar to the Armenian language, where *ors* means " teach," and also " shoulder."

† That *ethe* here means " when" or " if," was inferred by Dr. Donaldson from its position, and without the guidance of any linguistic resemblances.—*Varronianus,* p. 167 (2nd edition). This gives force to those resemblances which I have adduced.

Behistun ......*yatu, yathá* } "when."
Sanskrit ......*yadá*

12. *Erai,* "joyons," or " of joy."
Armenian *erah, khrakh, ovrakh,* "joyous, merry":
ovrakh linel, "εὐφραίνεσθαι" (Luke. xv. 24) : *kér, árb,
ev ovrakh ler, "φάγε, πίε, (καὶ) εὐφραίνου"* (Luke xii. 19).
Armenian *erakhan,* " a banquet." Cf. ἔρανος.
Erakhan would probably = *erah khan,* "joyous table,"
as *khan* means " table" in Armenian.

13. *Sie,* "it bo."
Armenian *izé,* " it be, it may be, may it be." A
comparison with the terminations of a Sanskrit
parasmaipada verb (*infra,* cap. v) tends to show that
the Armenian has preserved here the precativo form
of the substantive verb, and that the subjunctive
would be *ಶie*.
Sanskrit *syát:* Latin *sit* (= *siet*) : German *sei*.
Italian *sia.*

14. *Epana,* " the feast," nominative to *sie.*
Armenian *eph, ephovmn,* "cooking." Hebrew *aphah,*
"to cook." Latin *epulari.* Greek ὀπτάω, ἔψω, ὄψον.
For the termination of *ep-ana,* compare the Armenian
kap, "a bond," *kap-el,* "to contract," *kap-an,* "a
strait"—*gël-el,* "to roll," *gël-an,* "a cylinder"—
choh-el, "to expiate," *chah-anay,* " a priest." The
Armenian prefers to terminate words with *-ay,* instead
of *-a* simply. *Epana,* and also *kana (ante,* p. 83), are
just like in form to the Sanskrit *dána,* " gift."

15. *Mi,* "mo." See 1.
16. *Nethu,* " of liquor."

Armenian *nivth*, "substance, matter," *hetanivth*, "fluid substance, liquid," which are declined like *math* (6), and thus give in the genitive, dative, and ablative, *nivthoy* and *hetanivthoy*. *Nethuns* is the Etruscan form of *Neptunus*. As we have in Armenian *ivt* and *et*, "oil," and *girt* and *get*, "village," *nivth* would be very nearly *neth*, though the Armenian *iv* is usually pronounced like the German *ü*, and occasionally like the English *u* in *tune*. Compare the river-names *Neda* and *Nith*, and the Sanskrit *nadi*, "river."

17. *Nastav*, "the guest."

Armenian ...*nsdeh*
Persian ......*násti** } "stranger, foreigner."

Arabic ....*nazil*, "stranger, foreigner, visitor, guest."

Hebrew ......*nasa'*, "to migrate"; *nasa*, "to err."

---

* C. Calidius *Nasta*, "Strange, Guest," appears as a proper name in a Neapolitan inscription (Donati, p. 4), and *Nastes* is mentioned by Homer as one of the two Carian leaders. I have already noticed (*ante*, p. 85) that *Mestles* was an Etruscan proper name. It is a singular coincidence that the names, *Mestles* and *Nasta*, should be found in Italian inscriptions, one of them at Volterra, and that Homer, "Mæonii carminis ales," who would probably know what proper names were used in Lydia and Caria, should have written :—

and— Μῄοσιν αὖ ΜΕΣΘΛΗΣ τε καὶ Ἄντιφος ἡγησάσθην.

ΝΑΣΤΗΣ αὖ Καρῶν ἡγήσατο βαρβαροφώνων.

Lethe and *Lethi*, again, were Etruscan proper names (*ante*, p. 69); and Homer says that the Pelasgians at Troy were commanded by Hippothous and Pylæus,

υἷε δύω ΛΗΘΟΙΟ Πελασγοῦ Τευταμίδαο.

In Tuschi, *leth-* means "kämpfen, droben, schelten."

Sanskrit ......*neś*, "ire, se movere." *Nëś-deh* would be one who goes from his country (*deh*).

18. *Helephu*, "empties."

Armenian. $\begin{cases} zetovl, \text{ "to pour"}; zetkh, \text{ "drunken."}* \\ hetovl, \text{"to pour out, } \dot{\epsilon}\xi\epsilon\chi\epsilon\hat{\iota}\nu\text{" (Rev. xvi. 2).} \\ hetov, \text{ "he pours out, he empties."} \end{cases}$

The root is *het*, "pouring, flowing," which is found just above in *hetanivth* (16), where *nethu*, being qualified by *helephu*, acquires the meaning of *hetanivth* instead of *nivth*. The formation of *helephu* from a root *hel* may be thus illustrated from the Armenian :—

$\begin{cases} sós, \text{ "causing tremor" (root).} \\ sós\text{-}aph\text{-}il, \text{ "to tremble."} \\ thóth\text{-}aph\text{-}el, \text{ "to shake" (active).} \end{cases}$

ded-ev-el, "to reel."

$\begin{cases} khovs\text{-}el, \text{ "to fly."} \\ khovs\text{-}aph\text{-}el, \text{ "to fly."} \end{cases}$

$\begin{cases} śarź \\ sarsaph \end{cases}$ "a trembling."

$\begin{cases} śarźil \\ sarsil \\ sarsaphil \end{cases}$ "to tremble."

Similar forms are presented by *śóśaphel*, "to touch," *kachavel*, "to dance," and *śovthaphel*, "to hasten": so that *het'aphov*, as well as *hetov*, "he empties," might exist in an Armenian dialect.

Helephu is the last word in the Inscription of Cervetri. If all the Armenian words cited to explain this in-

---

* Cf. Thracian ζίλα, "*elśos*."—Bötticher's *Arica*, p. 50.

scription bo now collected together, and written in Etruscan letters, we should obtain in grammatical syntax, though the idiom might not be perfectly correct, the following Armenian couplet:—

*es mi ketu na es mathu mar em lezui tapean:
etho erah ize ephumn, zis nithu nesteh helu.*

Or, adopting such modifications as are warranted by the Armenian language itself—

*me mi ketu na me mathu mar em lezui tapurini:
ethe erah zie ephanay, me nithu nesteh helaphu.*

This distich differs but slightly from the Inscription of Cervetri, and almost entirely preserves the metre in which it is composed. Nor can it be said that the sense which the Armenian supplies for the Etruscan is at all forced or inappropriate; but, on the contrary, that it expresses exceedingly well what so festive a nation might have inscribed on one of their drinking-cups. For tho meaning of the two verses would be:—

1.

mi	I
ni	not
kethu	of water
ma	but
mi	I
mathu	of wine
mar	a cup
am	am
lisiai	for the tongue
thipurenai:	thirsty:

2.

ethe	if
erai	joyous
sie	be
epana,	the feast,
mi	me
nethu	of liquor
nastav	the guest
helephu.	empties.

The sentiment of the second verse brings to mind

Goethe's line on the drinking-cup of the King of Thule: *Er leert' ihn jeden Schmaus*. Some unimportant modifications might be suggested in the interpretation of the inscription. Thus *lisiai thipurenai* might be made a locative, "on (his) thirsty tongue," and connected with the second verse instead of the first. If, again, remembering that the Etruscan is several centuries older than the earliest existing Armenian, we compare the Etruscan *kethu, mathu,* and *nethu,* with the Sanskrit *madhu,* the Zend *mathu,* the Greek μέθυ, the Phrygian βέδυ, "water," and the Macedonian βέθυ, "nir" (both these last words being = Armenian *vivth,* "water, moisture, element, matter"), such analogies would lead us to consider the Etruscan words as nominatives or accusatives, rather than as genitives or ablatives. If they be in the accusative, then we should probably read, with Lepsius and Donaldson, *maram* instead of *maram;* and have to regard *maram* as a transitive verb of the second Armenian conjugation, like *tam,* "I give," or *ertham,* "I go," and signifying "I contain," or "I dispense." Compare the Albanian *marr,* "I contain," and the German *fass* and *fassen.* This alternation would have the advantage of obviating one little objection: for, if the Etruscan *sis* signify "it be," "I am" should rather be *em* than *am.* We have, however, both *am* and *is, wast* and *wert,* in English, where there is a similar change of vowel. If *nethu* be a nominative or accusative, *mi nethu* would be rendered "my liquor," or "my contents," *mi* being equivalent to "my" or "of me," both rendered in

Armenian by *im*. Finally, if *mi nethu* be a nominative, *helephu* would have a passive or neuter signification—the Armenian *zetov* is both active and neuter, like "pours" in English—and *nastav* would be in the instrumental case, and = Armenian *nśdehiv*. The instrumental cases of *nav*, "a ship," and *kin*, "a woman," namely *navav* and *knav*, come still nearer in form to *nastav*.

With these modifications the interpretation of the inscription would be: "I do not contain water, but wine: when there is a joyous feast, my liquor is poured out by the guest on (his) thirsty tongue." Perhaps this is on the whole the preferable interpretation of the two.

It does not require the knowledge of many sentences, nor of a large number of words and inflexions, to enable us to pronounce upon the character of any language; so that the properties of the Etruscan have probably been sufficiently displayed in the specimens already given and analysed, which seem to include all the forms whose meaning is tolerably clear. The result is that, instead of there being no language which can claim kindred with the Etruscan, there are, on the contrary, two in Asia which may succeed in establishing a near relationship to it by explaining it to a considerable extent. The Armenian appears to do this in a very close manner, especially when it is considered that Armenia and Etruria are at opposite extremities of a long and not entirely unbroken chain of old Thracian countries, like Wallachia and Portugal among those of Latin speech. It may even be said, perhaps, that the Armenian resembles the distant Etruscan more than it does the neighbouring Phrygian, with which it was connected by the ancients. But even if the Armenian had perished with the rest of the Thracian languages, of which only a few relics survive, yet the affinities between the Sanskrit and the Etruscan would still have afforded some clue to indicate who the Etruscans were. Their language would be nearly allied to the Sanskrit, but would nevertheless belong to a different Aryan family, as the letter-changes would imply. No doubt the Sanskrit has some few advantages over the Armenian in the comparison of languages. Thus the Etruscan *semph-*, "seven," is nearer to the Sanskrit *saptan* than it is to the Zend *haptan*, the Persian *haft*, or the Armenian *evthn;* and the Etruscan *sas*, "six," is nearer to the Sanskrit *śaś* than it is to the Armenian *wes̈*. But the Latin *septem* and *sex* are likewise nearer to the Sanskrit *saptan* and *śaś* than they are to the Greek ἑπτά and ἕξ; and yet the Latin and Greek are considered to belong to the same Aryan family of languages, while the Sanskrit and Latin are not so classed together. There are letter-changes which distinguish one Aryan family from another, as there are letter-changes which distinguish different members of the same family from one another. There is, besides, no letter-change in the case of the Armenian *wes̈* and the

Etruscan *sas*, as both would be ultimately derived, along with the Albanian *gyaś(të)* and the Persian *śaś*, from a form like the Zend *khsvas*, by the omission of different letters, after the manner in which the Old Norse *fimm* and the Anglo-Saxon *fíf* are deduced from the Gothic form, *fimf*. The argument from similarity or dissimilarity of numerals must not be pressed too far. Thus the Swedish *tio* and the German *zehn* have not one letter in common. The Gothic *fidvór*, too, resembles the Welsh *pedwar* more than the German *vier*: yet the Gothic was a Teutonic, not a Celtic dialect. The right conclusion would be, that the Gothic and Welsh forms are older than the German, as the Zend *thri* and the Etruscan *thr-* are older than the Armenian *ere*, "three." So, again, the Welsh *pump* and the Breton *pemp* are more like to the Gothic *fimf* than they are to the Gaelic *cuig*, as the Welsh *pedwar* and the Breton *pevar* are more like to the Gothic *fidvór* and the Anglo-Saxon *fcover* than they are to the Gaelic *ceathair*.* Nor is the advantage all on the side of the Sanskrit in respect of the Etruscan numerals. *Mach* (with *me-* and *muv-*), "one," is Armenian, but not Sanskrit; and the Armenian *hing*, "five," leads us from the Sanskrit *pańćan* to the Etruscan *kiem* or *chiem*.

It might be conjectured, on account of proximity,

---

* To get from *pemp* to *cuig*, we should pass through the Greek πέμπε and πέντε, the Lithuanian *penki*, the Armenian *hing*, and the Latin *quinque*. Greek and Oscan resemble Welsh, as Latin resembles Gaelic.

that the Etruscans were Illyrians rather than Thracians, if the Illyrians be supposed to constitute a distinct Aryan family. But, even if we set aside other arguments, and lay more stress than is allowable on numerals, there would yet be no necessity for such a conclusion, as the Albanian numerals hardly come nearer the Etruscan than the Armenian numerals do. Those are the Albanian numerals from 1 to 10: *nyë, dú, tré, katër, pesë,** *gyaś(të), śta(të), te(të), nën(dë), dhye(të)*. The corresponding Armenian numerals are: *ez* (and also *mi, mov,* and *mèn*), *erkov* (not Aryan), *er* or *ere(ch), ćor(ch)* or *char, hing, weš* (in composition *weś* and *wath*), *evthn, ovth, inn* (= *inën*), *tasn*.

Such advantages as the Sanskrit may have over the Armenian in some few instances cannot counterbalance the weight of evidence on the other side, so as to take the Etruscans out of the Thracian family. It is not to be expected that every Thracian language should be quite like the Armenian, any more than that every Teutonic language should be quite like the English, or that every Celtic language should be quite like the Welsh, or every Neo-Latin language quite like the French. And, while the Sanskrit explains so much of the Etruscan, it almost, by that very fact, disposes of its own claims to include the Etruscans in the Indian family. Such a word as *suthina*, for instance, if explained by the Sanskrit *hu*, "Diis offerre"—and a word found singly on votive offerings is perfectly so

---

* Compare the Lettish *peest*, which belongs to the same family as the Lithuanian *penkì*.

explained—is nearly decisive by itself. *Suthina* would not be a Sanskrit word; while, on the other hand, the Armenian brings out *suthina* from *hu* by presenting both the right letter-change, as well as the termination, in the word *zohorthivn*, "sacrifice." It enables us also to form such Etruscan words as *zilachnke* and *thipurenai* from Aryan roots, where other Aryan languages would not qualify us to construct them; and it has, in addition, the Etruscan *l* terminations, besides the singular Etruscan peculiarity of retaining in poetry the vowel which is discarded in prose. The Slavonian family of languages might compete with the Armenian on the ground of the letter-changes, but would fall far behind it, as well as behind the Sanskrit, in explaining Etruscan words. There is likewise a geographical improbability against the Sanskrit by reason of distance, and because Armenia fills up the gap between the Caucasian and Semitic nations.

The evidence in favour of the Armenian affinities of the Etruscan is not exhausted by the Etruscan inscriptions. For we find in Etruria place-names resembling the Armenian *sén* and *lori*, which may be described as the *town* and *home*, or *-ton* and *-ham*, of Armenia; as we find among Dacian plant-names terms like the Armenian *khot* and *det*, which are the *kraut* and *wurz* of Armenia. Finally, the Etruscan and Rhætian were said on sufficient authority to be cognate languages, and in Rhætia there are still apparent relics of an Armenian dialect; while in the Pyrenean *sern-eille*, "glacier," a similar dialect seems to have penetrated still farther west than Etruria. It can hardly be accidental that the only Thracian language still existing should emerge wherever the ancients have placed a Thracian people.*

---

* The quarter in which to look for the right language to explain the Etruscan was indicated by Bonarruoti a century and a half ago: "Hortari postremo fas mihi sit, doctos præcipue *linguis Orientalibus* viros, ut animi viros intendant, ad illustrandam veterem Etruscam linguam, tot jam seculis deperditam. Et quis vetat sperare, quod temporum decursu emergat aliquis, qui difficilem et inaccessam viam aperiat, et penetralia linguæ hujus reseret?" Niebuhr was less sanguine in his expectations. "People," he says, "feel an extraordinary curiosity to discover the Etruscan language; and who would not entertain this sentiment? I would give a considerable part of my worldly means as a prize, if it were discovered; for an entirely new light would then be spread over the ethnography of ancient Italy. But, however desirable it may be, it does not follow that the thing is attainable." And yet it has been known from the first that the ages of deceased persons were denoted in Etruscan by such forms as *avil ril* LXV, *ril leine* LV, and *lupu avils* XVII, which might, it would seem, have opened the way to the discovery, as they supply us with four words whose meaning can hardly be said to be doubtful, and which are thoroughly explained in every respect by the Armenian and Sanskrit languages.

CHAPTER V.

CONJUGATIONS AND NUMERALS.

It may be considered unnecessary to prove the Aryan character of the Armenian language by an analysis of the Armenian verb; so that the evidence in demonstration of the Etruscan being an Aryan lenguege of the Armenian or Thracian type might heve been closed with the interpretation of the Inscription of Cervetri. But the Armenians are even yet not universally admitted into the Aryan femily, although it is difficult to perceive on what grounds their right to such edmission hes been disputed; as their vocabulary, and, what is of more importance, their grammar also, are both decidedly Aryea. That their vocabulary is so in substance, the previous chepters may have sufficiently shewn; and in the present chapter I shall endeavour, by an exemination of Armenian conjngations, to complete the proof thet their grammar is so too. Albanian and Rhæto-Romance coujugetions will likewise be found compared with similer forms in other Aryan languages: and from these I heve passed to Caucasian and Basquo conjugations, in order to exemplify a little how far these languages deviate from the Aryan, and approach or differ from one another. Lastly, as the primeval population of Europe and Asia Minor may be conjectured (*ante*, p. 12) to have been composed of Caucasian, Basque, and Finnish elements, I have attempted to gain some insight into the obscure question of the relationship among these three races by an examination of their numerals. There are some indications of primeval affinity here which I have not found noticed, and which may appropriately bring this present inquiry to a termination.

Aryan Conjugations.
Present Indicative.

Lithuanian.	Sanskrit.	Rhæto-Romance.
esmi	asmi	sunt
essi	asi	cis
esti	asti	ei
esma	smas	essen
este	stha	esses
esti	santi	ean

Albanian.	Zend.	Behistun.	Armenian.
yam	ahmi	amiya	em
yê	ahi	.	es
ëstë	asti	astiya	é
yemi	hmahi	amahya	emch*
yini	stha		ech
ydnë	henti		en

---

* Here the Sanskrit -*mas* is converted into the Zend and Behistun -*mah*-, and the Armenian -*mĕch*, as we found (*ante*, p. 44) the Sanskrit *mâs*, "moon," converted into the Behistun *mâh*-, the Armenian *mah*-, and the Etruscan *mach*.

French.	Latin.	Italian.
suis	sum	sono
es	es	sei
est	est	è
sommes	sumus	siamo
êtes	estis	siete
sont	sunt	sono*

Imperfect Indicative.

Sanskrit (1st aorist).	Sanskrit.	Albanian.	Armenian (1st aorist).
adik-śam	ásam	yesë	sir-czi
-śas	ásîs	yese	-ezer
-śat	ásît	iś	-eaz
-śâma	ásma	yesëm	-ezach†
-śata	ásta	yesëtë	-ezich
-śan	ásan	iśnë	-ezin

Zend.	Behistun.	Armenian.
	áham	ëi
		ëir
ás	áha	ër
		ëach
		ëich
	áha	ëin

---

* Dante on two occasions uses *en* and *enno* for *sono*; forms which are like the Armenian *en* and the Rhæto-Romance *ean*.

† Here the Armenian omits the *m* of the Sanskrit and Albanian, but retains, under the form of *ch*, the final *s* which they drop. So, in the 2nd pers. plur., *t* is dropped, but *s* retained, in Armenian.

Sanskrit.	Zend.	Behistun.
abhavam	baôm	abavam
abhavas	bavô	
abhavat	bavaṭ	abava
abhavâma	bavâma	
abhavata	bavata	
abhavan	....	abava

Rhæto-Romance.	Albanian (aorist).
fova	kërko-va*
fovas	-ve
fova	-i
fovan	-uam
fovas	-ualë
fovan	-uanë

The root *bhu* or *fu* is not found in the Armenian language, which employs *li* or *eṭ* instead. This may account for there being no such words as *fuius* or *puia* in Armenian (*ante*, p. 60). In the Armenian first aorist, as in *sir-eżi*, "I loved," the *s* of the Sanskrit root *as* appears as *ż*, as it does also in the Armenian subjunctive. *Scrip-si*, (ἐ)φίλ-ησα (= ἐφιλέ-εσα), and *sir-eżi*, are analogous forms, all bearing a similar relation to the imperfect or preterite of the substantive verb that the corresponding form in Sanskrit does: and *-eżi* is to δί what *-εσα* is to ἦν, as may be readily seen when the Greek and Armenian forms are thus placed together:—

---

* *Kërkova*, "I sought," = Italian *cercava*, "I was seeking."

Greek.			Armenian.	
1st aorist terminations.	Impft.		1st aorist terminations.	Impft.
-εσα	-σα	ἦν	-ëzi	ëi
-εσας	-σας	ἦς	-ëzer	ëir
-εσε	-σε	ἦ	-ëaz	ër
-εσαμεν	-σαμεν	ἦμεν	-ëzach	ëach
-εσατε	-σατε	ἦτε	-ëzich	ëich
-εσαν	-σαν	ἦσαν	-ozin	ëin

In the imperfect of the substantive verb, both languages assume the augment (which lengthens the initial *e*), but drop, with one exception in each case, the sibilant of the root, which the Greek retains in the 3rd pers. plur., and the Armenian, under the form of *r*, in the 3rd pers. sing. The 2nd aorist, as well as the 1st, is formed from the imperfect or preterite of the substantive verb; and the manner in which it is done is again similar in Sanskrit, Greek, and Armenian; as may be exemplified by the 2nd aorist of "to place" in those three languages, to which a second form of the Albanian aorist is added:—

2nd Aorist.

Sanskrit.	Greek.	Armenian.	Albanian.
a-dh-âm	ἔ-θ-ην	e-d-i	plyak-a
a-dh-âs	ἔ-θ-ης	e-d-er	plyak-e
a-dh-ât	ἔ-θ-η	e-d	plyak-i
a-dh-âma	ἔ-θ-εμεν	e-d-ach	plyak-m
a-dh-âta	ἔ-θ-ετε	e-d-ich	plyak-të
a-dh-us	ἔ-θ-εσαν	e-d-in*	plyak-në

---

* Though there are two forms of the aorist in Armenian, yet no verb has more than one of them, except in the participle.

Sir-éï, "amabam," *sir-ezï,* "amavi," and *e-il-i,* "posui," exhibit the three preterite forms of the Armenian.

Present Subjunctive, Potential, & Precative or Optative.

Sansk. (subj.)*   Rhæto-Rom. (subj., pot. prec.)
syam   *seig*
syas   *scias*
syat   *seig*
syâma   *seian*
syata   *scias*
syan   *seian*

Sansk. (pot.)   Alb. (subj., pot., prec.)
yâm   *yém*
yâs   *yés*
yât   *yét*
yâma   *ycmi*
yâta   *yini*
yus   *yéne*

Sansk. (prec.)   Arm. (subj., pot., prec.)
yâsam   *izem*
yâs   *izes*
yât   *izé*
yâsma   *izemch*
yâsta   *izéch*
yâsus   *izen*

If we omit the *z* in these Armenian forms, we get the Sanskrit and Albanian potential; and if we trans-

---

* This and the two following forms are taken from a *parasmaipada* verb.

pose the *i* and *z̈*, the Sanskrit and Latin subjunctive, for *sim* = *siem*. The Armenian equivalent to the Latin *sit* would thus be *z̈ié*, = Etruscan *sie* (*ante*, p. 103).

The only Armenian future is a *futurum exactum*, like *scripsero* and τυφθήσομαι, being formed from the aorist by the addition of terminations which are modifications of the different persons of the subjunctive of the substantive verb; as *sirez̈-iz̈*, "amabo" (amavero), from *sirez̈-i*, "amavi." One of the following examples will exhibit a *first* aorist future of the *e* conjugation, and the other a *second* aorist future of the *i* conjugation: an Albanian aorist subjunctive is added, as being a form almost identical with the *futurum exactum* :—

Subjunctive.

sir-*iz̈em**	lin-*iz̈im*
sir-*iz̈es*	lin-*iz̈is*
sir-*iz̈é*	lin-*iz̈i*
sir-*iz̈emch*	lin-*iz̈imch*
sir-*iz̈éch*	lin-*iz̈ich*
sir-*iz̈en*	lin-*iz̈in*

Future.

sirez̈-*iz̈*	l†-*iz̈im*
sires-*z̈es*	l-*iz̈is*
sires-*z̈é*	l-*iz̈i*
sires-*z̈ovch*	l-*iz̈ovch*‡
sires-*ǵich*	l-*iz̈ich*, or -*iǵich*
sires-*z̈en*	l-*iz̈in*

---

* The subjunctive of the substantive verb is accurately preserved here throughout all the persons.

† The Armenian, like the Sanskrit and Greek, drops the conjugational *n* in the aorist and future.

‡ Cf. Armenian anoun = nomen.

Albanian Aorist Subjunctive.

plyak-śa or plyak-tśa
plyak-ś or plyak-tś
plyak-të
plyak-śim or plyak-tśim
plyak-śi or plyak-tśi
plynk-śinë or plyak-tśinë.

The Albanian tś, in the second of these forms, shews a tendency to convert the Sanskrit s into a sound resembling the Armenian ծ (tz) or ձ (dś). In the Armenian sireszes, etc., the z of sireźi becomes s. The Armenian and Albanian forms are both analogous in their terminations to the Sanskrit 2nd future:—

Sanskrit.

Subj. of "to be."	Subj. terminations.	2nd Fut. terminations.
syâm	-syam	-syâmi
syâs	-syas	-syasi
syât	-syat	-syati
syâma	-syâma	-syâmas
syâta	-syata	-syatha
syus	-syan	-syanti

The Armenian perfect is formed by combining the preterite participle with the present indicative of the substantive verb. For the participle compare:—

Armenian { sir-eal, "loved," or "having loved."
         { pah-eal, "kopt," or "having kept."

Old Slavonic by-t', "having been."

Mahratti pâh-ilâ, "seen" (cf. Dacian φιθοφθεθ-ελά; ante, p. 9).

And, for the perfect, compare:—

Armenian *sireal em*, " I have loved" (root *sir*).
Bengâli *kŏrilám*, " I mado" (root *kŏr*).*
Bohemian *byl sem* } " I was" (root *by*).
Polish *bytem*

An Armenian pluperfect, like *sireal éi*, "I had loved," i.e. "I was having loved," calls for no observation; and the same may be said of the imperative:—

Sanskrit.	Latin.	Armenian.
edhi	*es*	*er*
sta	*este*	*éch* or *erouch*.

CAUCASIAN AND BASQUE CONJUGATIONS.

Basque verbs are usually conjugated by combining a few auxiliary verbs and pronouns, united together in various agglutinate or incorporated forms, with the present participle, the preterite participle, and the future participle, of a particular verb. These participles are sometimes called infinitives. The Armenian *sireal em* and the French *aimer-ai* are modes of conjugation like those in Basque. Though Basque verbs have a strange appearance on account of the extent to which agglutination or incorporation is carried, yet they are simple enough when analysed. Thus *ecarri nézaque*, "je pouvais apporter," is quite plain when resolved into *ecarri n-éza-que*, "to-carry I-was-able"; *n-* being = *ni*, " I," *eza* the substantive verb, and *que* = Latin *que-o*. *Nézaque* is only "potoram" with the order of

---

* These analogies are derived from Bopp (*V. G.*, p. 1159). His argument, that *kŏrilám* "von participialem Ursprung zu sein scheint," would be strengthened by the Armenian *sireal em*, which is not agglutinate like *kŏrilám*.

the three elements reversed, as in the English "I was able." So again, *ecarri guinitzaiztzuque*, "nous to les pouvions apporter," is *ecarri guín-itz-aiz-tzu-que*, "to-carry we-them-were-to yon-able."

As personal pronouns present some of the most intimate signs of affinity between different languages, I shall endeavour to detach from these agglutinate forms the personal pronouns, or pronominal affixes, which are the subjects of the auxiliary verbs. It will be found that there is more than one such affix for each person, and that the Basque pronouns, in their present state, cannot explain several of the affixes. In the forms which I shall cite, all but the subjective affixes will be enclosed in brackets, so as to leave nothing but what belongs to the pronouns implicitly found in the Basque language; and I shall begin by placing the Basque *naiz*, "I am," between the Georgian *var*, "I am," and *machûs*, "I have." In both languages, as will be seen, the root of "being" has a common origin with the Aryan root; and this root takes three forms in Basque, as it does in the English am, art, is, ar(e).

Georgian.	Basque.	Georgian.
v(ar)	n(aiz)	m(achûs)
kh(ar)	(aiz), c(era)	g(achûs)
(ar)s	d(a)	(achûs, achûn)
v(ar)th	gu(era)	gv(achûs)
kh(ar)th	c(era)te	g(achûs)th
(ar)ian	d(ira)	h(chon)ian

There is a very clear resemblance here between

the Basque and the Georgian in the 2nd pers. sing.
and in the 1st and 2nd pers. plur. Four other Basque
conjugations are:—

n(uen)	n(uque)
(uen), cend(uen)	cend(uque)
z(uen), ce(uen)	l(uque)
guen(uen), guend(uen)*	guend(uque)
cen(u)t(en), cend(u)t(en)	cend(uque)te
z(u)t(en), cen(uen)	l(uque)te
n(ezan)	n(ioteque)
cen(ezan)	cen(ioteque)
c(ezan)	l(ioteque)
guen(ezan)	guin(ioteque)
cen(eza)te(n)	cin(ioteque)
c(eza)te(n)	l(ioteque)

Z-t(e), l-te, cend-te, and cen-te mark the plural of the
persons z and l, "he," and cend and cen, "thou," just
as we previously found in Basque, c(era), "thou art,"
and c(era)tc, "ye are"; and in Georgian, v(ar), "I am,"
and v(ar)th, "we are"; kh(ar), "thou art," and kh(ar)th,
"ye are."† In the Basque verbs cited above, the pronominal affixes were prefixed: in the verb which follows,
they are postfixed:—

---

* The d in guend- and cend- seems not radical, but phonetic or
euphonic. The sound of d rises between n and u, like that of p
between m and s, as in Sampson.

† Compare Ossetic forms like lag, "man," lagthā, "men"; ye,
"he," yethā, "they." The Ossetic plural suffix is -thā or -the
(Sjögren, p. 52).

(de)t
(de)c, (de)n, de(zu)
(de)u
(de)gu
(de)zue, (de)zute
(de)ue, (d)ute

These pronominal affixes, with the addition of the actual Basque pronouns, will give us the pronominal forms contained in Basque for " I, thou, he, we, ye, they." But, before they are compared with Caucasian and other forms, it is advisable to mention the complete Georgian form for "I." The pronoun itself is *me*, but the genitive *čemi*, as well as the other cases of the pronoun, shew that *čem* is another or a more perfect form, just as *šen*, "thou," makes *šeni*, "of thee." The Aryan analogies to the Basque will suggest themselves without notice. The Basque pronominal forms are:—

"I."
- ni } Hungarian *én*; Suanian *noi*, "we, *nos*";
- n- } Lesgi *niśe*, " we."
- -t. Tuschi *so*, -*s*.
- *Ten* or *teni* may be the complete Basque form.
- Lesgi *den*, *tun*;* Georgian *čem(i)*; Lazic *škim(i)*.

"Thou."
- hi. Tuschi *ho*, -*h*.
- zu, -zu. Suanian *si*. Greek σύ.
- c-, -c. Georgian *kh-*, *g-*.
- -n } Georgian *sen*; Turkish *sen*;
- cen-, cin- } Lazic *skan(i)*.
- The complete Basque form might be *zchuen*.

---

* There are several Lesgi dialects. My authority for them is Klaproth's *Kaukasische Sprachen*.

"He, this, that."
$\begin{cases} a, au, o \\ -u \end{cases}$ Tuschi o; Turkish o; Abkhasian ui.
ce-, c-. Georgian igi; Lesgi heyen, gen. hegei.
z-. Turkish śu.
l-. Turkish ol; Lesgi il; Spanian alle.
d-. Esthonian ta; Lapponic ta(t).
There would be more than a single form here.

"We."
$\begin{cases} gu, gu-, -gu. \text{ Georgian } gv\text{-; Tuschi } wai, \text{ thcho;} \\ \quad\text{Lazic śku.} \\ guen-, guin-. \text{ Georgian } \text{\'even}; \text{ Lazic } \text{śkun(i).} \\ \text{Guen seems plainly the complete Basque form.} \end{cases}$

"Ye."
$\begin{cases} zue(c), -zue, -zute. \text{ Tuschi } śu, -ś. \\ c—te. \text{ Georgian } kh—th, g—th. \\ cin-, cen-, cen—te. \text{ Georgian } thchven, \text{ Lazic} \\ \quad tqua, tquan(i). \\ \text{The complete Basque form seems nearly } zeuen. \end{cases}$

"They."
$\begin{cases} aie(c), oie(c), -ue. \text{ Lesgi } hai, hoi, ua, \text{``this.''} \\ \left.\begin{array}{l} -ute \\ z—t \\ c—te \end{array}\right\} \text{See under ``ho.''} \\ \left.\begin{array}{l} l—te \\ l- \end{array}\right\} \text{Turkish } -l(or); \text{ Lesgi } il, \text{``ho.''} \\ d-. \text{ Lapponic } tah; \text{ Lesgi } ti. \\ con-. \text{ Georgian } igini; \text{ Lazic } hini. \end{cases}$

Assuming *ten, zchuen, guen,* and *zeuen,* as the complete or primitive Basque forms for "I," "thou," "we," and "ye," some suggestive comparisons may be made between the Aryan, Caucasian, and Basque languages:—

Greek ...... ἐγών
Sanskrit ... aham
Zend ...... azem
Behistun ... adam   "I," = ah(am).
Lesgi ...... den
Basque ... ten
Georgian . ćem
Lazic ... .. śkim

Zend ...... tûm
Behistun ... t'huwam
Sanskrit ... tvam   "Thou," = tv(am).
Basque ... zchuen
Lazic ...... skan
Georgian ... śen

Tuschi ...... wai
Behistun ... wayam
Sanskrit ... vayam
Zend ...... vaém
Basque .. guen   "We," = vay(am).
Georgian ... éven
Lazic ... { śkun / śku
Tuschi ...... thcho

Sanskrit ... yûyam
Zend ...... yûżem
Basque ... zcuen
Georgian ... thchven   "Ye," = yûy(am).
Lazic . { tquan / tqua
Welsh ...... chwi
Tuschi ...... śu

Although the Caucasian and Basque languages are far from being Aryan, yet it seems as if there were some ancient connexion between the three forms of speech. There may have been some group of men in Western Asia, from which the Basques first broke off, and then the Caucasians; while the remainder, or at least a part of the remainder, subsequently moulded their language into the primitive Aryan, which became subject to different modifications when the Aryan race spread abroad, and became divided into families, and subdivided into nations. For it is with the most ancient Aryan forms that the Georgian and Basque languages appear connected by their pronouns. The Georgian *th-chve-n* and the early Basque *z-cue-n*, "ye," must be older than the Welsh *chwi*, "ye," if allied to it; and the Georgian *č-ven* and the Basque *g-uen* seem even more ancient than the Sanskrit *vayam*, "we," though the Tuscbi *wai* would be a younger form. If the resemblances in the cases of "we" and "ye" justify us in identifying the Georgian and Basque termination -*en* with the Sanskrit termination -*am*, then we should have a right to apply the same principle to "I" and "thou." Here then the Caucasian and Basque would retain signs of a characteristic which is only found in the most ancient Aryan languages: "Den ausgang -*am* in *aham tvam*, *azem túm*, entbehren alle jüngeren sprachen" (Grimm). Yet we find in Caucasian dialects *den*, *čem(i)*, and *škim(i)*,—*šen* and *skan(i)*, for the singular of the first two personal pronouns, and can construct from the Basque, *ten*, "I," and *zchuen*, "thou."

One more resemblance between the Caucasian and the Basque is worth notice. It may be seen from such forms as *jangó nu-que*, "que je mangerais," when compared with *ecarri néza-que*, "jo pouvais apporter," that the Basque conditional or potential is formed by the suffix *que*, implying "ability." The subjunctive is formed in a similar manner by the suffix *lá*. Thus we have:—

"venio," *natór*	*natorrelá,*	"veniam."
"venis," *atúr*	*atorrelá,*	"venias."
"venit," *datór*	*datorrelá,*	"veniat."
"venimus," *gatóz*	*gatorrelá,*	"veniamus."
"venitis," *zatózte*	*zatocelú,*	"veniatis."
"veniunt," *datóz*	*datoztelá,*	"veniant."

The subjunctive is formed exactly in the same way in Tuschi by the suffix *le*, which is referred by Schiefner to the verb *la(ar)*, "to wish." Cf. λá-ω. In Tuschi, *do* is "facit," and *dole* is "faciat," like as in Basque *dator* is "venit," and *datorrelá* is "veniat." The conditional in Tuschi is formed by the suffix *he* or *h*: as *dahe* from *da*, "ho is," and *doh* from *do*, "he does." In Lesgi we have *bugo*, "er ist," and *bugabi*, "es sei."

NUMERALS.

It has been said by Grimm, in the chapter of his *Geschichte der Deutschen Sprache* which is devoted to the subject of original affinity (*urverwandschaft*): "Mit recht hat man drei kennzeichen ermittelt, welche in sämtlichen urverwandten sprachen, wo nicht unverändert, doch höchst deutlich und eigenthümlich anzutreffen sind, und füglich als symbol derselben aufgestellt werden dürfen. Ich meine die übereinkunft der *zahlen*, *persönlichen pronomina*, und einzelner formen des *substantiven verbums.*" Conjugations and personal pronouns I have already examined as evidences of early affinity; and now, by the aid of such a comparison and analysis of numerals as I am able to make, I shall endeavour to penetrate a little further, if possible, into the difficult subject of the original relationship of the Basques, the Fins, and the Caucasians, the three races by whom Europe was probably peopled at the time when the Aryans first entered it. It will not be necessary to set down Aryan numerals, as they are so well known: the others which I shall notice are these:—

	I	II	III	·IV	V.
		Finnish.			
Fin	*yksi*	*kaksi*	*kolmi*	*neljä*	*wiisi.*
Esthonian	*üts**	*kats†*	*kolm*	*nelli*	*wiis.*
Lapponic	*akt*	*qwekte*	*koln*	*nelje*	*wit.*
Syrianic	*ötik*	*kyk*	*kujm*	*njolj*	*vit.*
Hungarian	*egy*	*kettö*	*három*	*négy‡*	*öt.*
		Basque.			
	bat	*bi*	*hirú*	*lau*	*bost.*
		Caucasian.			
Georgian	*crthi*	*ori§*	*sami*	*othkhi*	*khuthi.*
Tuschi	*zha*	*si*	*qho*	*dhew*	*phchi.*
Circassian	*se*	*tu*	*si*	*ptl'e*	*t'chu.*
Abkhasian	*aka*	*vi*	*khi*	*phsi*	*chu.*
		Turkish.			
	bir	*iki*	*úć*	*dúrt*	*beš.*

* Genitive, *ütts*.   † Genitive, *katte*.
‡ Compare these Finnish numerals for "four" with the Tamil *nángu, nálu,* "four."
§ Compare the Chinese *ér,* "two."

THE OLD ITALIANS. 131

	VI	VII	VIII	IX	X.*
		Finnish.			
Fin	kuusi	seitsen	kahdeksa	yhdeksa	kymmen.
Esthonian	kuus	seitse	kattesa	üttesa	kümme.
Lapponic	kut	kictja	kaktse	aktse	lokke.
Syrianic	kvajt	sizim	kōkjamys	ōkmys	das.
Hungarian	hat	hét	nyoltz	kilentz	tiz.
		Basque.			
	sei	zazpi	zortzi	bederatzi	amár.
		Caucasian.			
Georgian	ekhvsi	śvidi	rva	ękkra	athi.
Tuschi	yetlich	wort	bart	iss	itt.
Circassian	chi	b'le	ga	bgu	pśe.
Abkhasian	f'	biś	au	· ś'	śva.†
		Turkish.			
	álti	yédi	sékiz	dókuz	ón.

The first point to which I would draw attention here is, the manner in which several of these numerals for "eight" and "nine" are formed. It will be at once apparent, on comparing the Fin, the Esthonian, and the Lapponic expressions for "one" and "two," "nine" and "eight," that in each of the three dialects the last element of "nine" and "eight" is the same, while "ono" is the first element of "nine," and "two" of "eight."‡ Thus, in Esthonian, "ono" is üt(s), and

---

* Observe, as a basis for inquiry, that the decade comprises only three characters, "one," "five," and "ten." The Fin kak-, the Syrianic kyk, and the Turkish tki, "two," seem = yk yk, II.

† The non-radical Abkhasian suffix -la is omitted throughout (ante, p. 52).

‡ Cf. Pott, Zählmethode, p. 129, note.

"nine" is *ūt-tesa;* "two" is *kat(s),* and "eight" is *kat-tesa.* The only solution of this is, that such numerals for "eight" and "oine" are formed on the principle of the Roman IIX and IX, *duodeviginti* and *undeviginti;* ond consequently that in the Fin -*deksa,* the Esthonian -*tesa,* ond the Lopponic -*tse,* we have three forms of a word allied to the Aryan for "ten," which is, besides, found explicitly in the Syrianic *das,* "ten" (= Ossetic *das* or *düs*), and io the Hongarian *tíz,* "ten." Precisely in the some manner the Syrionic *kŏkjamys,* "eight," and *ŏkmys,* "nine," oro formed, and would therefore imply a word *mys* or *amys,* "ten," which the Syrianic *komyn,* "thirty," *neljamyn,* "forty," and *vitymyn,* "fifty," would indicate to exist olso under the form *myn, amyn,* or *ymyn.* This word seems to me the Fin *kymmen* and tho Esthonian *kümme,* "ten," and may be akin to the Basqoe *amár,* "ten," which takes the form *ama* in *ama-icá,* "cleven," where *icá* would ho "one," and = Sanskrit *eka,* Abkhasian *aka,* Hungorian *egy,* etc.

The Huogorian ood Basque for "eight" and "nine" would likewiso be compound terms, but of a different nature. As we can hardly avoid connecting *nyol-* in the Hungarian *nyol-tz,* "eight," with the Finnish words for "four," such as tho Syrianic *njolj* and the Lapponic *nelje,* it would follow that *nyol-tz,* "eight," most = 4 × 2 (compare *quatre-vingt*), ond consequently that -*tz* is equivolent to *two, zwei,* or the Tuschi *si,* "two." In *ki-lentz,* the Hungarion for "nine," I should conjecture thot *lentz* is the same as *neltz* or *nyoltz,* ond that *ki-len-tz* = 1 + 4 × 2.

The next step is to compare the Hungarian and the Basque for "eight" and "nine":—

Hungarian.		Basque.	
"One,"	*egy*,	*bat*,	1.
"Eight,"	*nyol-tz*,	*zor-tzi*,	4 × 2.
"Nine,"	*ki-len-tz*,	*bed-era-tzi*,	1 + 4 × 2.

The Hungarian and the Basque seem here to have the same formation, but to possess only one element in common, which is *tz* or *tzi*, "two"; and, as the Basque for "two" is *bi*, which is to be compared with the Latin *bi(s)* and the Abkhasian *vi*, the Basque would apparently contain a complete form for "two" very nearly identical with the German *zwei*, = Sanskrit *dvi* or *dva*. So we have in Hindustani, *du*, "two," and *bâ*-reh, "twelve." Again, the Basque forms for "eight" and "nine," if they are composed like the Hungarian, would contain *zor* and *era*, "four." These elements, too, may be allied to the Aryan, as "four" is in Sanskrit *čatvâr* or *čatur*, in Afghan *ẕalûr*, in Hindustani *čâr*, in Armenian *čor* and *char*, in German *vier*, and in Swedish *fyra*. R is the letter which is retained in every Aryan form of "four."

When we pass from the Pyrenees to the Caucasus, and consider the Georgian for "eight" and "nine," this letter *r* immediately attracts attention. For, in the Georgian language, "eight" is rva_1 and "nine" is *zkh-ra*, which last form = 1 + 8; for *zkh*- would = Tuschi *zha*, "one," and -*ra* would = *rva*, "eight."

The comparison between the Basque and Caucasian numerals for "one," "eight," and "nine," leads to these results:—

Circassian ...*ſe* ⎫
Lesgi ....*zn*   ⎬ I.
Tuschi ....*tha* ⎭

Georgian...... *r — va* ⎫
Suanian....... *ar - a* ⎬ VIII.
Mingrelian ... *r — uo* ⎭

Georgian......*ekh-r — a* ⎫
Suanian ......*ékh-ar - a* ⎬ IX.
Mingrelian ...*ékh-or - o* ⎭

Basque...... ⎧ *but,*   I.
             ⎨ *zor-tzi,*   VIII.
             ⎩ *bed-era-tzi,*   IX.

Using the term "Iberian" to include the Georgian, Suanian, and Mingrelian dialects, it may be said with great probability :—

I. In Iberian and in Basque, as in Hungarian, "eight" $= 4 \times 2$, and "nine" $= 1 + 4 \times 2$.

II. Of the three elements, "one," "two," and "four," which compose "eight" and "nine," "one" is different in Iberian and Basque, while "two" and "four" are the same, and are apparently Aryan as well as Basque and Caucasian: for the Caucasian *r-*, *ar-*, and *or-*, with the Basque *zor-* and *era-*, may all be referred to Aryan forms for "four"; and the Caucasian *-va*, *-a*, *-uo*, and *-o*, with the Basque *-tzi*, may all be brought out of such Aryan forms as *dva*, *duo*, and *zwei*. Indeed, the Aryan for "two" is explicitly found in Caucasian and Basque; as "two" is *tu* in Circassian, *si* in Tuschi, *vi* in Ahkhasian, and *bi* in Basque; so that the Georgian *-va*, "two," in "eight," is nearly Basque, and the Basque *-tzi*, "two," in "eight," is nearly Tuschi.

III. The Hungarian contains the Aryan for "two," under the form -*tz* in "eight"; and the Hungarian, with other Finnish dialects, contains the Aryan for "one" and "ten" also.

All this seems as if there were a certain bond of connexion between the three races that preceded the Aryans in the West, the Basques, the Fins, and the Caucasians; and likewise as if these three races and the Aryans had in very remote ages a common ancestry and a common home.*

There are other signs in Basque of the use of numerals which are not explicitly found in that language. Thus "après demain" is in Basque *etzi*, which may be akin to the Georgian *ze-g*, "après demain," where *-g* is perhaps to be compared with the Georgian *dghe* or the Basque *egun*, "day." Again, in Georgian, *mazeg* is "en trois jours"; and, in Basque, *etzi-damu* is "en trois jours," and *etzi-dazu* is "en quatre jours." Here the Georgian *ma-zeg* appears to signify "one after-to-morrow," while the Basque *etzi-da-mu* and *etzi-da-zu* appear to signify "after-to-morrow and one," "after-to-morrow and two." If so, then *zu*, "two," is implicitly contained in Basque; and *mu*, "one," and *ma*, "one," are implicitly contained in Basque and Georgian, and are to be compared with the Armenian *mi*, *mov*, *me-*, "one," and the Etruscan *mach*, *me-*, *muv-*, "one." *Da* means "and" in Georgian,

---

* The Tamil *on-badu*, IX, is formed like the Fin *yh-deksa*, "one from ten," out of the Tamil *onrru*, I, and *pattu*, X; as the Tamil *aindu*, V, and *pattu*, X, coalesce into *aim-badu*, L.

as *eta, ta, enda, da*, do in Basquo. *Etzi-da-mu* and *etzi-da-zu* would be formed like the Basquo *oguei-tabat*, "twenty and one," and *oguei-t(a)-amar*, "twenty and ten, thirty." The Georgian for "thirty" is a similar form, *ozda athi = ozi-da-athi*, "twenty and ten." The difference between the Basque o-*guei* and the Georgian o-*zi*, "twenty," is similar to that between the Latin vi-*ginti* and the Armenian ch-*san*, where the Latin *g* is changed for a sibilant. Both -*guei* and -*zi*, as well as *o-*, might be Aryan.

The following Aryan numerals seem thus to have been detected in Caucasian, Basque, and Finnish:—

"One"—in Finnish as *yk, ki-*, and *egy*; in Basque as -*icá*; in Caucasian as *aka*.

"One"—in Caucasian as *ma-*; in Basque as -*mu*.

"Two"—in Caucasian as *tu, śi, vi, -va, -a, -uo,* and *-o*; in Basque as *bi, -tzi*, and -*zu*; in Finnish as -*tz*.

"Four"—in Caucasian as *ar-, -or-,* and *r-*; in Basque as *zor-* and *-era-*.

"Ten"—in Finnish as *tiz, das, -deksa, -tesa,* and -*tse*; and possibly in Caucasian as -*zi* (= *tsi*), and in Basque as -*guei*.

The analysis of numerals is worth prosecuting farther. The most perfect Aryan form for "six" is the Zend *khsvas*, otherwise written *csvas*, which would have passed into *khvas* before it could give the Armenian *wez* and the Albanian *gyaś(té)*. Now *khvas* is like the Georgian *ckhvsi*, "six," but gives no explanation of it. If, however, we interpret *ckh-vsi* by the Finnish dialects, it becomes significant. It would be *yk-wiisi*,

1 + 5, and = Fin *k-uusi*, Esthonian *k-uus*, "six"; which, with the three other Finnish forms for "six," may likewise be reduced to 1 + 5, VI. Having got thus far, let us again take up the Zend *kh-svas*, and suppose it, as well as the Ossetic *ach-sűz*, "six," to be 1 + 5. In this case, *svas*, with the Sanskrit *śaś* and the Afghan *śbaź*, "six," would properly be "five"; just as the Armenian *wez*, "six," having lost the prefix implying "one," is to be compared with the Fin *wiisi*, the Lapponic *wit*, the Turkish *beš*, and the Basque *bost*, all signifying "five." In like manner, as we have seen (*ante*, p. 54), the Circassian *chi*, VI, would be the Etruscan *ki* and the Lesgi *chewa*, V; the Etruscan *huth*, IV, would be the Georgian *khuthi* and the Lazic *khut*, V; and the Ahkhasian *phśi*, IV, would be the Tuschi *phchi*, V. It seems, then, as if there were once a primeval word, *svas*, "five," which was common to Aryans and Turanians; and this word would be found in Basque with its original sense, as the second element of the Basque *zaz-pi*, VII, would be the Basque *bi*, II: for *zaz-bi* would become *zazpi*, just as *ez*, "non," and *ba*, "si," coalesce in Basque into *ezpa*, "nisi." It is evident, if *zazpi* be VII, and *pi* = *bi*, II, that *zaz* must necessarily be V, though this would have been forgotten when terms like the Sanskrit *śaś* were employed for "six." The adoption of a new term, such as *pańćan*, for "five," may have been the cause of such inaccuracy.

Signs of primeval affinity seem so remarkable here as to deserve being tabulated :—

Hebrew ....*echad,*............... I.
Hungarian ......*egy,* .... I.
Sanskrit ....*eka,* .... I.
Abkhasian ......*aka,* .... I.
Chinese .... *wù,* ...... V.
Lapponic...... { · *wit,* ...... V.
k——*ut,* ...... VI.
Esthonian ... { *wiis,* ...... V.
k——*uus,* ...... VI.
Georgian.........*ekh*——*vsi,* ...... VI.
Armenian ...... *wex,* ...... VI.
Ossetic............*ach*——*sāz,* ...... VI.
Basque......... { *bi,* II.
zoz——*pi,* VII.
Hebrew .... *šēš,* ...... VI.
Sanskrit .... *šaš,* ...... VI.
Zend ....*kh*——*svas,*...... VI.
Afghan .... *šbaz* ...... VI.
Turkish .... *beš,* ...... V.
Basque .... *bost,* ...... V.

Have we any indications of what this supposed primeval word for "five" may have been? There cannot be much doubt about the most probable meaning for such a word. This meaning is "hand": and the apparent affinity between such words as the Persian *panj,* "five," and *panč,* "fist," has been noticed by several writers. The Basque *bost,* "five," might thus be related to the Slavonic *pjast,* "pugnus," and to the German *faust* and the English *fist;* all which words have nearly the termination of the Zend *zasta,*

Sanskrit *hasta,* "hand." So too the Turkish *beš,* "five," which seems akin to the Basque *bost,* "five," resembles the Gaelic *bas, bos,* "the palm of the hand," which is the same word as the Welsh *bys* and the Breton *bez,* "finger"; terms capable, like the Armenian *boyth,* "thumb," = Welsh *bawd,* of explaining the Basque *bat,* "one," and perhaps the Turkish *bír,* "one." In like manner, we might pass from the Tuschi *bui,* "fist," to the Chinese *wù,* "five." It may, too, be possible that both the Turkish *beš* and the Basque *bost,* "five," are originally allied to the Afghan *šbaž,* "six" (properly "five"), and to the supposed primitive *svas,* "hand." At any rate, a word like *svas,* "hand," seems contained in many languages of different families. It may emerge in the Armenian *thath,* "hand, fist"; in the Tuschi *tot,* "hand"; in the Egyptian *toot,* "hand"; in the Gaelic *dòid,* "hand"; and again in the Armenian *thiz,* "a span," *thëz-ouk,* "a pygmy." It may be seen (*ante,* p. 105) how *sûs* = *thóth* in Armenian. *Svas* may also appear, and in a form more like itself, in the Persian *sâž,* "make"; in the Armenian *šóš(aphel),* "to handle"; in the Phrygian *sos(esait),* "he makes"; and in the Gaelic *sàs,* "lay hold of." A similar word might be discerned in the Basque *escú,* the Suanian *ši,* and the Chinese *šeù,* all signifying "hand": and even the Esthonian *kässi* and the Lapponic *kät,* "hand," the Lesgi *koda,* "hand," the Ossetic *koch, kuch,* "hand," *kach,* "foot" (cf. Armenian *kach*-avel, "to dance," and English *kick*), and the Tuschi *k'hak,* "hoof," may bear some signs of an original likeness to *svas*, which has become the Welsh *chwech*, "six, ἕξ." The Lapponic *kät*, the Lesgi *koda*, and the Ossetic *kuch*, "hand," would help to explain the Georgian *khuthi*, "five," like as the Georgian *phekhi*, "foot," is apparently identical with the Tuschi *phchi*, "five." The Circassian *t'chu*, "five," and *pśe*, "ten," seem allied to *khuthi* and *phchi*; and if so, then the Circassian *pśe* would be "feet," as the Abkhasian *śva*, "ten," might be "hands." Reckoning by scores originated, most probably, in men once counting with their feet as well as their hands. Both Caucasians and Basques reckon by scores: thus "forty" is "twice twenty," and so on. The apparent identity of the Abkhasian *śva*, "ten," with the Basque *zaz-*, "five," in *zazpi*, "seven"; and of the Georgian *phekhi*, "foot," with the Tuschi *phchi*, "five," the Abkhasian *phśi*, "four" (properly "five"), and the Circassian *pśe*, "ten";—this shews how "ten" may be the plural of "five," and thus be nearly the same word. We may consequently compare the Tuschi *itt*, the Lazic *wit*, the Mingrelian *withi*, and the Georgian *athi*, all meaning "ten," with such Finnish words for "five" as the Lapponic *wit* and the Hungarian *öt*. The Finnish words might originally signify "hand" or "foot," and the Caucasian words, "hands" or "feet."

The five Finnish expressions for "six," *kuusi*, *kuus*, *kut*, *kvajt*, and *hat*, are all alike, and all probably $= 1 + 5$. But, in the expressions for "seven," a difference is discernible. The Lapponic *kietja* and the Hungarian *hét*, "seven," may $= 6 + 1$; but the Fin *scitsen*, the Esthonian *seitse*, and the Syrianic *sizim*, "seven," seem differently composed, and bear a likeness to the Georgian and the Basque for "seven":—*

    Fin ....*soi-tse(n)*.
    Esthonian ...*sci-tse*.
    Syrianic ......*si-zi(m)*.
    Georgian ......*śvi-di*.
    Mingrelian ...*sqwi-thi*.
    Basque.........*zaz-pi* (= *zaz-bi*, 5 + 2).

There is no objection to making *sci-* = *si-* = *śvi-* = *zaz-*, as *se-decim* = *sex-decem*, and *śo-daçan* = *śaś-daçan*. Similar instances of elision may perhaps be found in the Hebrew *śéś*, *śe-ba'*, and *śe-mónch*, "six," "seven," and "eight."†

Svas, "hand," especially as we have also the Basque *escú* and the Suanian *śi*, "hand," as well as the Abkhasian *śva*, "ten," i. e. "fives" or "hands," will thus bring together the Basque *zaz-* (which is nearly *svas*), and the Georgian *śvi-* (which preserves the *v* of *svas*, and is like the Abkhasian *śva*), and the Mingrelian *sqwi-* (which approaches to the Basque *escú*), and the Syrianic *si-* and the Fin *sei-* (which resemble the Suanian *śi*). In like manner, the Aryan *dva*, *dvi*, *zwei*, *bi(s)*, and δί(ς), with the Tuschi *śi* and the Abkhasian *vi*, "two," will explain the Basque *-pi* (= *bi*), and the Mingrelian *-thi*, and the Georgian *-di*,

---

* It is worth noticing, by the way, that *scitse-n* and *sisi-m* have terminations like the Aryan *sapta-n* and *septe-m*.

† *-mónsh* seems allied to *mánsh*, "part, number," and *múnsh*, "part, time." "Parts" imply duality at the least.

and the Syrianic -*zi*, and the Fin -*tse*; which last two forms would thus = the Hungarian -*tz* in *nyol-tz*, 4 × 2, and *ki-len-tz*, 1 + 4 × 2, as well as the Basque -*tzi* in the similarly composed numerals, *zor-tzi* and *bed-era-tzi*.* The Abkhasian *bi-ś*, "seven," may contain the elements, *bi*, "two," and *ś*, "five," = Suanian *śi*, "hand." In the Georgian, Abkhasian, and Basque, and in the three Finnish dialects, the Syrianic, the Esthonian, and the Fin Proper, there would consequently appear to be a similar combination of the same two elements in the number VII; and these elements would belong to the ancestors of the Aryans, as well as to the ancestors of the Fins, the Caucasians, and the Basques. These last three families or nations would, moreover, when they formed their "seven," have used *svas* rightly, as "five," not as "six." This cannot be said of the Aryans: for if the Sanskrit *sa-pta*(*n*) is connected with *śaś* (which may possibly be the case, though the Zend *khsvas* and *haptan* seem

---

* The explanation of the Finnish *sci-tse*, "seven," as 6 + 1, from such forms as the Basque *sei*, "six," and the Circassian *se*, "one," might be possible, but would hardly be probable. In another Finnish dialect, the Ostiak, *ki* is II (= Syrianic *kyk*), *vet* is V (= Syrianic *vit*), and *ta-vet* is VII, i. e. *ta* + V. Therefore *ta* is II, as well as *ki*, which is used *subtractively*, as in *kyt*, III, i. e. *ki*, II, from *vet*, V. *Ta-vet*, VII, is thus formed out of the same elements as the other Finnish, the Caucasian, and the Basque terms for VII (p. 141); elements that are Aryan as well as Turanian. The Ostiak *kyda*, VI, seems = *kyt-da* (= *ta*), 3 × 2; as *nida*, VIII, would be *nət-da*, 4 × 2, like the Hungarian *nyoltz*, the Basque *zortzi*, and the Georgian *rva*. The Ostiak *nət*, IV, seems = "one from five (*vet*)," as the Tamil *nángu*, IV, seems = "one from five (*aindu*)."

against such a supposition), yet we could not well get "two" out of -*pta*.* If "two" is found at all in coalition with *śaś*, it would rather be in *aś-ṭa(n)* or *aś-ṭau*, "eight." *Aś* is "six" in Lazic, and *sa* is "six" in (Pelasgic) Etruscan. As in the Georgian and Basque pronouns, so too in the formation of the Georgian and Basque for "seven," an affinity to the language which was becoming Aryan would appear, though the three forms of speech became afterwards very distinct.†

It may have been observed that Finnish dialects

---

* Compare the Circassian *pt-l'o*, "four," which seems = "one from five," ɪv. The Aryan numerals for "three," "four," "seven," and "eight," are not easily explained. "Four" is perhaps the most difficult.

† Dr. Latham, in his *Varieties of Man* (p. 127), gives the word *khut*, "hand," as used in the Manipur and Khoibu languages in Upper Birmah; and he compares it with the Lesgi *koda*, "hand." It is still nearer to the Georgian *khuthi* and the Lazic *khut*, "five," and to the Pelasgic Etruscan *huth*, "four." *Svas*, "hand, five," does not appear to be confined to the Old World, for I find in the same work the following Natchez words:—

i-spesh-e, "hand."
shped-oo, "five"

Spesh and *shped* may = *svas*, as Armenian *spit-ak* = Sanskrit *çvet-a* = English *whit-e* = German *weiss*; analogies which shew how the Natchez *shpedee*, the Lapponic *wit*, and the Fin *wiisi*, all meaning "five," may be originally the same word. Compare also *ispeshe*, "hand," with the Sanskrit *spaç*, "facere," and the Gaelic *spdg*, "paw." Again, "hand" is *shag-al* in Omahaw, and *shak-e* in Mohawk; and "foot" is *see* and *seeh-ah* in Sioux, and *a-shoo* in Pawnee. *Su* is "foot" in Chinese. At Norton Sound, near Behring's Straits, "hand" is ai-*shet*, "nails" are *shet-ooo*, and "four" is *shet-amik*. We may have here, and in the words cited in the text (*ante*, p. 139), different forms of one of the primitive words of the human race, and a sign of its original unity.

employ in composition a different word for "ten" than their own (p. 132). So does the Etruscan in *-lchl*, "*-genti*," = *lch-lch*, 10 × 10. So does the Lithuanian in *-lika*, "*-teen*," = Polish *lik*, "number." And so, too, does the English in *e-leven* and *twe-lve*, the Gothic *ainlif* and *twalif*. Grimm agrees with Bopp in regarding *-lif* (and *-lika*) as forms of a primeval word for "ten," *einer uralten zehnzuhl*. This word seems to be found, and in our English form *-leven* too, in the Malay *sa-lapan*, "nine," and *du-lapan*, "eight"; words which contain the Malay *sa*, "one" (cf. Circassian *se*, Lesgi *za*, Tuschi *sha*, "one"), and *duwa*, "two" (a perfect Aryan form like the Afghan *duva*), and are evidently constructed just like the Fin *yh-deksa*, "nine," and *kah-deksa*, "eight," IX and IIX. As the Malay is thus connected in some points with more western and northern languages, it is possible that it may be so in other points, and thus be allowably employed in the explanation of such languages. Now the Malay for "five" is *lima*. Prefix to this the *kah*, "two," of the Fin *kah-deksa*, "eight," = 2 from 10, and we should obtain *kah-lima*, 2 from 5, "three," which might be contracted into the Fin *kolmi* and the Lapponic *kolm*, "three," nearly as *two-leve* becomes *twelve* in English. The Finnish words for "four," such as the Esthonian *n-elli*, may mean "1 from 5," IV, and be allied to the Turkish *ál-ti*, "six," *élli*, "fifty," and *él*, "hand." If the Etruscan *za-l* and the Georgian *sa-mi*, "three," are allied to the Fin *ko-lmi*, and thus imply *sa-lmi* as a more perfect form, then *za* and *sa* would be "two," like the Tuschi *śi* and the German *zwei*. Compare also the Javanese *tá-lu*, "three." At any rate, since there are several ways, as will be more completely shewn directly, of making -*l* = "five," the Etruscan *za-* in *za-l* would most likely be "two," and thus = Georgian *sa-*; for it seems that the Georgian *sa-mi* = Mingrelian *su-mi* = Lazic *ǵu-m* = Syrianic *ku-jm* = Lapponic *ko-lm*, "three," i. e. "*two* from five." And thus the composition and the first elements of the Etruscan *za-l*, and the Georgian *sa-mi*, "three," would apparently be the same, whatever may be thought of their second elements. If *t* be "five" in the Tuschi *wor-t*, "seven," and *ba-r-t*, "eight," then *wor-* and -*r-* would be "two," = Georgian *ori*, = Chinese *âr*; while *ba-* would be "one," and probably allied to the Basque *bat*, "one," and possibly to the Hebrew -*ba*' in *śe-ba*', "seven." As the Tuschi *ba-rt*, "eight," seems = 1 + *wort*, "seven," so the Circassian *b-gu*, "nine," may = 1 + *ga*, "eight," as the Georgian *skh-ra*, "nine," = 1 + *rva*, "eight." It is difficult to guess what the Circassian *gu* or *ga*, "eight," may have been originally; but, if we were to combine it with the Georgian *rva* and *ra*, "eight," we might get *g-r*, "four," and *ua* or *va*, "two." The Circassian would, however, in such a case, want the characteristic letter *r* of the Aryan "four"; and the Abkhasian *a-a*, "eight," if = 4 × 2, would have suffered still more than the Circassian *g-a*.

It may be as well to tabulate for the second, or *l* "five," as I have done for the first (*ante*, p. 138) :—

L

Welsh	{ bys,	"finger."
	llaw,	"hand."
Breton	bez,	"finger."
Cornish	lau,	"hand."
Armenian	boyth,	"thumb."
Turkish	êl,	"hand."
Malay	{ lima,	"hand."
	lima,	v.
Basque	{ bat,	I.
	bi,	II.
Tuschi	ŝi,	II.
Georgian	ori,	II.
Chinese	ár,	II.
Fin	ko — lmi,	IIV (ko- = "two").
Syrianic	ku — jm,	IIV.
Lazic	ģu — m,	IIV.
Mingrelian	su — mi,	IIV.
Georgian	sa — mi,	IIV.
Etruscan	za — l,	IIV.
Javanese	tû — lu,	IIV.
Circassian	pt————l'e,	IV.
Esthonian	ne————lli,	IV (ne- = "ono").*
Syrianic	nju————lj,	IV.
Basque	lau,	IV ("one" lost).
Circassian	b'——le,	VII.
Tuschi	{ wor—t,	VII.
	ba————r——t,	VIII.

The Abkhasian bi-ŝ and the Circassian b'-le, "seven,"

---

* See also note (ante, p. 142), and compare Tamil nâlu, IV (ante, p. 130, note). Nýë is "one" in Albanian.

appear similar forms, with the same "two," and a different "five." $Bi\text{-}\acute{s} = 2 + 5$, as the Basque *zaz-pi* and the Georgian *śvi-di* = 5 + 2. The Malay *lima*, "five," is evidently the *lima*, "hand, arm," of the islets between Timor and Papua.* Like the former word for "five, hand," this second word seems to stretch across Europe and Asia. For, as the Basque *escu* would be the Suanian *śi* and the Chinese *śeu*, all meaning "hand" (as the English *skew* and *shy* are the German *scheu*), so the Malay *lima*, "hand," "five," and *-lapan*, "ten," are to be compared with the following words cited by Diefenbach (*Lex. Comp.* s. v. *lofa*) : Gothic *lofa*, "the open hand," = Scotch *loof;* Gaelic *làmh*, Welsh *llaw*, "hand"; Cornish *lof, lau*, "hand"; Gaelic *lapadh*, "paw"; Polish *łapa*, "paw"; Lapponic *lapa*, "the sole of the foot." The same root would also be found in the Welsh *llam*, "stride, step," and in the German *lauf* and the English *leap;* as well as, probably, in the Tuschi *lap*, "step, stair, treppe," and *lam*, "mountain." By a similar association of ideas, we may connect together the Tuschi *it*, "run," and *itt*, "ten"; and might detect *svas* in the Hebrew *śûś, śîś*, "rejoice, leap" (cf. Polish *sus*, "hüpfen"), *sûs*, "horse," and *sâs*, "moth," = σῆς. *Svas* might also supply the thema for the Armenian *sôs*- or *thôth*-, *śovth*- and *kach*-, as well as for *śóś*- (p. 105). Of the three characters which compose the decade, I, V, X,

---

* Crawfurd's *Malay Grammar and Dictionary*, vol. i, p. xcviii. Cf. Pott, *Zählmethode*, p. 121.

the most likely meaning for I is "finger"; for v, "hand"; and for x, "hands" or "fingers" collectively. The English *ten*, *-teen*, as the German *zehn* and *zehen* intimate, is " toes," i. e. " fingers";* and *-leven* would probably be "hands." The resemblance which the Circassian *so*, Lesgi *zu*, Tuschi *zha*, " one," bear to the German *zehe, zeig-*, and *zeich-*, or to the Basque *atz*, "finger," should perhaps not be passed unnoticed.

The Polynesian dialects are connected with the Malay family. The following numerals are used in Hawaii and Tahiti†:—

	I	II	III	IV	V.
Hawaii...	*akahi*	*arua*	*akoru*	*ahaa*	*arima*.
Tahiti ...	*atahi*	*arua*	*atoru*	*amaha*	*arima*.
	VI	VII	VIII	IX	X.
Hawaii...	*aono*	*ahitu*	*avaru*	*aiva*	*umi*.
Tahiti ...	*aono*	*ahitu*	*avaru*	*aiva*	*ahuru*.

Rima means "hand, arm," in Hawaii, just as *lima* does in Malay; and thus explains the Polynesian *arima*, " five," as the Malay *lima*, " hand, arm," does the Malay *lima*, " five." The Polynesian initial *a* seems superfluous. There is a similar conversion of *l* into *r* in the Finnish dialects, where the Esthonian and Lapponic *kolm*, " three," becomes the Hungarian *három*, " three," which may enable us to pass to the Basque

---

* " Noch unleugbarer stehn δάκτυλος, *digitus* und *seha* (digitus pedis) mit *δέκα, decem, δέκατμμ* und *zeigen* in zusammenhang."— Grimm, *Geschichte der Deutschen Sprache*, p. 244.

† These islands are separated by 2500 miles of sea.

THE OLD ITALIANS. 149

hirú, "three." Compare, too, the Hindustani so-*leh*, "sixteen," and set-*reh*, "seventeen."* The Polynesian words for "three" are plainly "1 to 2," and not "2 from 5" like the Finnish. The Hawaiian *umi,* "ten," resembles the Fin *kymmen* and the Esthonian *kümme,* "ten," as well as the Basque *amár* or *ama,* "ten." The Polynesian *arua,* "two," is rather like the Georgian *ori* and the Chinese *ár,* "two"; and the Polynesian *ava-ru,* "eight," might possibly be compared with the Georgian *r-va,* "eight," supposing the two elements reversed, as well as with the kindred Suanian and Mingrelian terms for "eight," *ara* and *ruo.* The Lazic *ovro,* "eight," is still nearer to *avaru.* Such resemblances should be mentioned, though I hold to the former explanation of *rva, ara,* and *ruo* (*ante,* p. 134). *Avaru* seems = 4 × 2, and is thus apparently composed like the Hungarian and Basque for "eight," though with different elements.†

---

* *L* is always represented by *r* in Zend. The city of *Lima* in Peru is so called from the river *Rimac.*

† The Malay *laki,* "man, husband," may be compared with the following words:—Circassian *lay,* "flesh"; *lay, t'hlay,* "blood"; *tlay,* "husband";—Ossetic *lag,* "man"; *lappu, latu,* "lad";—Lesgi *les,* "man"; *less,* "husband"; *il'yadi,* "wife";—Lycian *lade,* "wife"; —Abkhasian *lkhadza,* "husband";—Esthonian *laps, lats,* "child." The Caucasian *Leges* and *Lazi* of antiquity were probably the "men." *Olaks* means "man" in the Arawak dialect of Guiana, which supplies an example of "numeration of the rudest kind," where *kabo* is like the Tamil *kai,* "hand." See also p. 139.

Aba da kabo = "once my hand," = *five.*
Biama da kabo = "twice my hand," = *ten.*
Aba olaks = "one man," = *twenty.*

(Latham, *Ethnology of the British Colonies,* p. 260).

With regard to the symbols, ɪ, v, x, "the digit," "the hand," and "the hands" or "the fingers," ɪ would represent accurately enough tho extended finger, and v the angular space between the thumb and the forefinger when the hand is held up. This angular space is called in Armonian *chil*, which is like the Georgian *kheli* or *qheli*, "hand"; both which terms might contain the Etruscan or Pelasgian *ki*, "five," with the addition in one case of the Etruscan and Armenian termination -*il*, and in tho other of the Georgian termination -*eli*. x would be the figure formed by placing tho two hands across one another. The Chinese character for "ten" is a cross, which is called *śi*, as "hand" is called *śeù* in Chinese, and *śi* in Suanian, and as "ten" is *śva* in Ahkhasian.

The results of the previous analysis of numerals are to be taken in conjunction with what seems to follow from tho numbers on the Etruscan dice, namely, that the *Pelasgic* Etruscan numerals were Caucasian. See especially the tabular view (*ante*, p. 54). The inferences which I should be inclined to draw from the numerals, as well as from conjugations and pronouns, have been already explained in my first chapter, where I have brought together several other coincidences of different kinds, which appear by their combined force to conduct us to a similar conclusion. And this conclusion would be:—that before the Aryans began to spread from their original home, they dwelt there with Fins and Caucasians on their west; the

Caucasians tending towards the south, and the Fins towards the north: and that as the Fins scattered themselves, speaking in a general manner, over the northern half of Europe, the Caucasians did the same over the southern half, but probably at an earlier period; for the Caucasians, especially if it were allowable to include the Basques among them, cannot be said to have developed a common numeral system before dispersion, while the Fins would have done so, though not quite as perfectly as the Aryans. Both of the Turanian races would have been continually impelled farther westward, as the Dravidas would have been southward, by the expansion of the Aryans, who ultimately broke through the Western Turanians by two different routes, one on each side of the Euxine, and gradually encroached upon them till they were left as they now are, in the Caucasus, and the Pyrenees, and the North of Sweden and Russia, though their ancient presence in the heart of Europe is still indicated by two or three words used in the Alps. When Livy attributed Etruscan affinities to the Alpine population in general, but especially to the Rhætians, he probably spoke with more accuracy than has been generally thought, or even perhaps than he himself was aware of. For all, or nearly all, the original inhabitants of the Alps (as well as of the pile-dwellings on the Swiss lakes) may have been *Tuscan*, i.e. Caucasian, while the Aryan *Rasenæ* penetrated no farther to the west than Rhætia, and a subsequent Celtic inroad made the Aryan population of Noricum quite as much Celtic as

Thracian. In Armenia and the Caucasus, Asia may thus claim both elements of the Etruscan people as her own, whether they were of Tyrrhenian or of Pelasgian origin. Such, at least, is the hypothesis which seems to explain all the evidence that I have brought forward, and to solve at the same time four ethnological problems. In ancient ethnology, we are led to ask, who were the Etruscans, and who were the Pelasgians? and, in modern ethnology, what has become of the two races of which the Armenians and the Caucasians are the surviving representatives? Each pair of questions supplies the answer to the other pair.

INDEX OF ETRUSCAN WORDS.

Achrum, "Hades, Acheron," 87.
Alpan, "supplex," 78, 91.
Am, "sum," 100: or see s. v. *mar*.
Avenks or *(Ap)avenks* } "deponit, reliuquit," 38.
Avil, "ætas," 27, 28, 30.
Avils, "ætatis," 27, 33, 37.
Chiem, "quinque," 49.
Chimths, "quindecim" (?), 49.
Chiseliks, "monumentum, μνήματα," 79, 92.
Eka, "hic, ecce," 61, 87, 90.
Epana, "epulum," 103.
Erai, "hilaritatis," or "hilaris," 103.
Erske, "sese offert," 87.
Etera, "alter," 59.
Ethe, "si, quando," 102.
Fleres, "oblatio, donum," 79, 80, 86.
Flerl (qu. *flersl*), "oblatum, datum," 86.
Puius, "υἱός," 60.
Helephu, "effundit," or "effunditur," 105.
Huth, "quatuor," 51, 54.
Kana, "simulacrum," or "statua," 83.
Karutezan, "quatuordecim" (?), 49.
Kealchls, "quingentos," or "quingentesimi" (gen.), 41, 43.
Kecha, "expiat," or "solvit," 78, 80, 90.
Ken, "ut," 79.
Kepen, "tumulum," 36 (note).
Kerinu, "sculpit," 90.
Kethu, "aquæ" (gen.), or "aquam," 97, 107.
Ki, "quinque," 51, 54.
Kiemzathrms, "quinquagesimi tertii," 39.
Kis, "νεκρός,"—or else "menses," or "mensis" (gen.), 47.
Kisum, "νεκρόν," 47.

M

Kiri, "νεκροῖς," or "νεκρός," or "moritur," 47.
Klalum, "mœrorem, funera," 37 (note).
Klan, "soboles," or "princeps," 59.
Klen } "pius, rite," 78, 70, 80, 89, 90.
Klensi }
Krer, "soror," 89.
Leine, "vivit, fit," 27, 28, 29.
Lenache, "facessit, fieri facit," 91, 92.
Line, "vivebat, vixit," 29, 69.
Lisiai, "linguæ" (dat.), 100.
Lthas, "λιτῆς," 78, 80, 91.
Lupu } "obit, moritur," 33, 37.
Lupuke }
Lupum, "cadaver, corpus," 37.
Lusni, "luminis," 94.
Ma, "sed," 99.
Mach, "unus, 51.
Machs, "mensis" (gen.), or "menses," 41, 44.
Mar, "vas, fass," 100: or else —.
Maram, "contineo, ich fasse," 107.
Mathu, "vini" (gen.), or "vinum," 99, 107.
Mealchls } "centum," or "centesimi" (gen.), 41, 42, 43.
Muvalchls }
Mi, "ego, me," 60, 80, 97, 99, 103.
Nak, "ad, nach," 87.
Nastav, "hospes," or "hospite," 104, 108.
Nesl, "mortuus," 61.
Nethu, "liquoris," or "liquorem," 103, 104, 107.
Ni, "non," 97.
Puia, "filla, θυγάτηρ," 60.
Puiak, "figliuola, θυγάτριον, töchterlein," 60.
Puiam, "filiam," 60.
Puil, "τέκνον," 60.
Rasne, "ulna," 49.
Ril, "annus," 27, 28, 30.
Sa, "sex," 51.
Sak }
Sech } "proles," 60.
Sek }
Salthn, "fusio, fusum, τόρευμα, opus," 94.
Sansl, "libens," 79, 88.
Sas, "sex," 38.
Semphalchls, "septingentos," or "septingesimi" (gen.), 41, 43.
Sie, "sit," 103.

INDEX OF ETRUSCAN WORDS.

Suthi, "conditur," 61.
Suthi
Suthik } "sepulcrum, tumulus," 69, 90.
Suthina, "θυσία," 83, 84.
Teke, "facit," or "ponit," 79, 91.
Tenine
Tenu } "tenet, tendit, fert, offert," 79, 90.
Tesne, "decem," 49.
Tesnsteis, "centum," 49.
Thapna, "καυστηρ, lampas," 94.
Thipurenai, "calidæ, sitienti," 101.
Thu, "duo," 51.
Thuf
Thup } "τύπος, signum," 78, 80, 91.
Thui, "memoratur," 69.
Thunesi, "diei," 42, 45.
Tinskvil, "Jovi(s) donum," 93.
Tiers or tivrs, "triginta," 38, 39.
Tlen-achais
Tlen-asies } "debitum pretium, meritum," 78, 86.
Tular, "sepulcrum," 63.
Turke
Turuke } "dat," 80, 87.
Tuthines, "gratiæ, χάριτες," 78, 79, 83, 84.
Via, "filia," 60.
Zal, "tres," 51, 55.
Zek, "statua," 88 : or perhaps zeke, "affert."
Zilachnke
Zilachnuke } "infoditur, sepelitur," 34, 36, 47.

THE END.

www.ingramcontent.com/pod-product-compliance
Lightning Source LLC
Chambersburg PA
CBHW030250170426
43202CB00009B/694